PRAISE FOR DEFEND
THE DEFENSELESS

Defend the defenseless is such a good book! It is a great book, the product of a beautiful mind. It is a lot more than a child caught in a war. It is so much more than a father's request to his beloved daughter. It is a collection of sublime thoughts on a Nation's tragic past and uncertain future, but by an educated and cultured mind shaped by a loving and well nurtured childhood. The reflection does not really pass judgment or make unfounded conclusions, there is no hidden agenda. It is a narrative that speaks beyond the parochial interests of ethnic group, state or nation and seeks the higher ideals of social justice.

Dr. Anthony Akenzua
Consultant Psychiatrist, Oxleas NHS Foundation Trust, England

Defend the defenseless is terrific! I could take only one break reading it.

Lou T. Wells,
Author and Lecturer
Herbert F. Johnson Professor of International
Management, Emeritus, Harvard Business School

I could not put this wonderful book down. I learned so much about the period of the Biafran war in Nigeria's history. I feel that through the author's beautiful writing I know her family, especially her mother, and her comforting assurances that things would be all right, through so much fear and hardship. Defend the defenseless comes alive for me.

Carolyn Newberger,
Clinical and research psychologist, artist, flutist, and essayist

To
Katie Getchell,
Thank you for being the
wonderful kind person
that you are .....
Best wishes
Arese Carrington

DEFEND
THE
DEFENSELESS

A MEMOIR

ARESE CARRINGTON

Defend the Defenseless

Published by
Bronzeline & Co. Publishing
ISBN: 978-0-9995043-3-8
Library of Congress Control Number: 2017957425

A father's love for his children,
A mother's bravery,
Love crossing all boundaries,
Hate building all boundaries,
Hopes dashed,
Faith conquering,
Humanity at its best and worst,
The tragedy of war,
The rhapsody of peace
A nation in need...

THIS BOOK IS DEDICATED TO:

Hannah, my grandmother whose wisdom
still guides me till this day

Elisha and Dora, my parents whose love, warmth and
bravery helped me survive the trauma of war,

Walter, my husband and soul mate

Temisan, my very own...

DEFEND THE DEFENSELESS
ACKNOWLEDGEMENTS
AND APPRECIATION

My special gratitude goes to:

My daughter, Temisan, like your name, may good always be yours, for you have brought so much goodness into my life.

My husband Walter, for the bond that we share and your shining example of courage and integrity.

My siblings who support my endeavours by being there for me.

To everyone who has made this book possible through oral historical accounts, advice and support or who has positively impacted my life.

Thank you to all my friends for their interest.

To my friend Michael Feldberg for your unwavering support for this book.

"This memoir is not intended to open up sore wounds but to help us navigate our way by remembering our history so we can project into our future."

TABLE OF CONTENTS

PART ONE

NIGERIAN CIVIL WAR

CHAPTER ONE

LAGOS...A sheltered child, an innocent childhood.

L AGOS IN THE NINETEEN SIXTIES, a bustling city proud
of Nigeria's newly acquired independence. Nigeria, which
began as a geographic entity arbitrarily assembled by the
British during the colonial era had become Africa's most populous
country. As its capital, Lagos had become a progressive city. Its
people were proud to be *omo ekos* (Lagosians). 'Highlife' (a music
genre characterized by Afro- Cubano rhythms originating in
Ghana) was the music of choice. Colorful traditional outfits were
worn with great pride. Nigeria's future seemed bright.

So soon after independence, there were still remnants of the
colonial structures. The civil service set up under the British
remained in place, but no one minded because it was an excellent
civil service and Nigerians themselves were now in charge. They now
had a chance to rise to the top without colonial masters breathing
down their necks. Those British individuals who remained in the
civil service had to give Nigerians the respect they deserved. The
Nigerian people had pride and discipline.

My father had studied engineering at the University of London
and was a chief engineer in the Waterworks section of the Public
Works Department (PWD). He quickly rose in rank to an Assistant

Director in the later formed Ministry of Works and Housing. He was proud to be a civil servant.

My mother, who had studied nursing and midwifery at Queen Charlotte's Hospital at Hammersmith in England, was now a full-time housewife, taking care of my six siblings and me. Her nursing background proved useful in caring for seven children.

We lived in an exclusive part of Lagos called Ikoyi, as did most civil servants and their families. It was a beautiful, safe suburb, with big houses and large compounds filled with casuarina shrubs and fruit trees. Ikoyi was filled with tree-lined streets, street lights and well paved roads. It was where the British had lived before they hauled down the Union Jack and gave us back our independence. I was a kid then, carefree, playing with my friends and brothers and sisters on the streets, riding bikes on the streets, a bit of a tomboy, climbing trees…not a worry, not a care and all so ready to act on any dare.

In our compound, there was a building tucked away at the back, completely hidden behind shrubs and a wall. The colonialists called it the "Boys' Quarters" and it was used to house their servants. I remember the big mango tree with its massive trunk that towered above our two-storey home. I was told the tree was over one hundred years old. There were also almond trees in our back garden. I always looked forward to the fruit season because hundreds of fruit would fall off the trees and we could eat as many as we wanted. My siblings and I would dry the seed, crack it open and eat fresh raw almonds. They tasted good and were nourishing.

On Saturdays, my parents had the night out. My mother would dress up gorgeously in a traditional outfit called "Up and Down." I assumed the outfit was called "Up and Down" because it had a top piece and a bottom piece. The top was usually tight fitting and short sleeved and sometimes had an intricate pattern in front with the zipper or buttons always at the back. The bottom was usually a long fitted skirt made of the same fabric as the top or a long wrapper made of a fabric called "George." When my mother was going on her Saturday night outings with my father she would wear her "Up and Down" with a long fitted skirt. For formal functions she would wear it with a double layer of "George" wrapper and an intricately tied "Haze" head tie. Occasionally, she would wear a long maxi gown with embroidery round the neck and front. I loved helping her get ready. My parents made a handsome couple. Mother loved getting ready because her husband was taking her out to dance the highlife at the rave of the time, Caban Bamboo Night Club with the famous singer, Bobby Benson. Those were the days, life was sweet and everything seemed certain. That was the Lagos in the sixties I like to remember. Everything good seemed to be happening; I saw enthusiasm, hope, and pride in the faces of the adults. It seemed nothing could possibly go wrong.

As a child, I did not comprehend the rumblings of political unrest. With independence came decisions that involved the country's destiny as it moved forward, especially the division of power among the diverse Nigerian peoples who the British had formed into one geographic entity. The British had handed power over on October 1, 1960 in such a way that political control was vested in the country's North and exercised by the Prime Minister, Tafawa Balewa. The mostly ceremonial role of President went to the veteran independence leader, Nnamdi Azikiwe from the Eastern Region. Now the future of the country lay in their hands along with those of the other founding fathers, who represented the nation's various regions, ethnic groups, clans and religions. The euphoria of independence was fading and, with the colonial masters out of the way, the nation's different ethnic groups began to look at and suspect one another. They, however, momentarily seemed to keep it all together. I was a child, so at that time I did not know the details. I later found out about the subsequent coups that led to what I had dreaded most: civil war, which shattered the innocence I once knew.

During the mid to late sixties I attended private school in Ikoyi. I had many friends at school, many of whom were expatriate children. After school, I loved to have my friends over or go and visit them. I seemed to be the social butterfly amongst my siblings. One of my closest friends was from Palestine and another was from Israel. Although they did not seem that close to each other, I thought nothing of it.

Parents liked to know where their children were, and whenever I went to a friend's house a driver and the nanny would have to drop me off, and later pick me up at the agreed time. One Saturday, I had gone to visit my Palestinian friend. She lived in an apartment building in Southwest Ikoyi. I remember that day clearly. She was happy to see me. We played "hide and seek." When it was my turn to hide, I opened a door in the kitchen pantry and was stunned to see a room full of cans of food, water and different supplies. It looked like a supermarket. We never kept that volume of supplies in my house. We went to the stores and market to buy food when we ran out. I remember my mother went to the supermarket almost every day. Why, I wondered, did my friend's parents have this store full of food and bottled water?

I forgot about playing hide and seek. I had to know right away. Instead of her finding me, before she could call out "Ready or not, here I come," I found her. I took her to the store room and asked her for an explanation.

Our families were of similar economic status, so I questioned why they had a store of supplies and we did not. My friend looked at me and took me to a corner as if she was about to tell me a secret she was not meant to know. She looked into my eyes, and said in a low voice, "I overheard my parents and some of their friends talking. They said 'the winds of war are in the air.' Apparently, when those winds arrive they bring severe shortages of food and water, so we have to prepare. We left Palestine because of war and now, in Nigeria, my parents think another war is about to come." My friend looked deeper into my eyes as if she was searching for some comfort from my soul and said, "Why does war follow me around? My parents say if war breaks out in Nigeria we will have to move again to another country."

Although I was stunned, I replied her reassuringly, "There is no war about to break out." I knew my parents would tell me if that were the case. We too, would have a store full of supplies. Any playful spirit left, I was no longer myself, the certainty and innocence I felt left me. I needed to get home; I needed some answers from my parents. I needed reassurance. How could I be so uninformed when I always seemed to know everything happening even though I was a child?

As soon as the driver, Mr. Taiwo, came to pick me up, I jumped into the car and asked, "Is it true there is going to be a war in the country?" Mr. Taiwo was taken aback by the question. He quickly said to me, "You are a child, what concerns a child with war? Just keep playing like a child." That was not good enough an answer for me. I needed to hear from my parents. As soon as I got home, I jumped out of the car. I ran upstairs, forgetting to knock on the door, as I barged into my parent's room. My parents were there. I expected my mother would be getting ready for her Saturday night out with my father, but neither of them looked like they were going out.

I began to talk nineteen to the dozen, bombarding them with questions about a war.

Is a war about to break out in our country?

Why didn't you tell me?

What will happen to us if there is a war?

Can we go one hundred years without a war?

My friend told me about the war and her parents have a food supply room, so why don't we have one?

Questions, questions, questions kept flooding my mind, as it was working non-stop like a clock. I was confused and scared and I needed to know.

My mother finally pulled me close as she saw the anxiety on my face. She put my head on her chest and tried to reassure me that "everything will be fine." My father said he would talk to the family as a whole after dinner with all the children present.

No one had denied any of the questions I had asked. I knew it must be true. After all, it was unusual for my parents to stay at home on a Saturday night. I closed my eyes in fear, I felt the world was changing around me.

Our house was a large white colonial two-storey building. Upstairs there were four bedrooms, the room I slept in with my sisters was a later addition built when a new dining room was added. There was a wooden upright chair on the stairway landing where I often sat. I would gaze out through the window, which overlooked a roundabout on the driveway that led to the gate. It was my favorite spot for day-dreaming during the war that was to come. Downstairs in the entryway was a "No Smoking" sign boldly written in red and white. My parents were totally against smoking and lectured us never to smoke. The entryway led to the main living room, which we called the parlor. In the center of the room was a large, masterfully carved wooden lion with a gaping large mouth and sharpened ivory teeth. My younger siblings and I were told by the nanny that if we put our hands in the lion's mouth it would bite off our fingers. I can still recollect that there was a period when I suspiciously looked at the lion and avoided being in close proximity to it. The floor of the parlor was made of beautiful oak wood, which was polished once a month using Mansion polish and buffed with half of a coconut husk. This routine became less frequent during the war because many commodities became scarce, including floor polish. The windows were low and I remember jumping in and out through them till my father had burglary proofing grates installed. Our night watchman, Baba Beji, had asked my father to do that to prevent thieves from climbing in. Baba Beji was a bold, friendly older man who had fought in Burma during the Second World War. His battle front experience would later make him my 'encyclopedia' on war. He carried around a bow and arrow as well as a sword. Although he did not have the physique of a U.S. marine, he had the confidence that he could tackle any intruder that came into the premises.

Adjacent to the parlor was a dining room, its floor and those of the other rooms were made of terrazzo. We did not have carpeting anywhere. My father felt it was more difficult to keep clean and, with the hot climate would accumulate more dirt and harmful bacteria. My father had a phobia of germs. He loved the pristine beauty of wood, terrazzo and marble on floors.

The dining room was an addition to the house that sat beside the former, smaller dining room that was now used as an informal sitting area. The former dining room was too small for our long dining table and was visible from the entranceway. My parents wanted a room big enough to fit all of us children and cousins who would sometimes spend vacations with us. They also wanted it separate from the living room and more private. My siblings and I had assigned seats at the table. My father sat at the head, my seat was on the right hand side of my father and my mother's seat was on his left. I remember my father once saying my mother's seat was on the left of his because that seat was closest to his heart. No one was allowed to sit in my mother's seat. That precedence may be why even now as an adult, at the dining table, when my husband sits at the head of the table, I sit on his immediate left.

Before dinner my father or someone else, would pray, saying, "Bless this food Oh Lord for Christ's sake." However when my younger sister or I prayed we loved to sing, "Thank you for the world so sweet/Thank you for the food we eat/Thank you for the birds that sing/Thank you God for everything."

That night at dinner, with a war pending, I did not think the world was so sweet. My father said the prayer blessing the food that night. I could barely eat. I just wanted dinner to be over. With what I knew, how could I eat? My other siblings sat at the dinner table;

there was the usual noise, jokes and story-telling. I was usually one of the loudest, but today I was quiet. I looked at my siblings and wondered. They did not know what was happening. A war was about to break out! They would not laugh and joke if they knew what I knew. The meal seemed to take forever. Finally, my father said we should all gather in the living room, he would like to talk to us.

He told my brothers and sisters what I had found out. A war was about to start and as a family we must prepare and have a plan. My mother and father then continued to expand on what was happening as gently as they could so we would not be overcome with fear. They said the war probably wouldn't get to Lagos. It would most likely be concentrated in the eastern part of the country. It was still all a probability and things might resolve themselves so we should not worry. I kept quiet throughout till the end. I then asked if we were going to store up food supplies. My father said my mother would go out to buy non-perishable foods in bulk starting the next day. My father then told all of us to follow him. We looked at one another and wondered what he was up to. We lined up behind him and were led to a large space underneath the staircase. He said structurally that space was the safest if a bomb were to drop on the house. He was an engineer, after all, so he should know. He explained to us that in case of a bomb attack, we should not panic. A siren would go off. If it happened at night we should put off all the lights in the house and lie flat, side by side, under the staircase with our hands over our heads. He said another siren would go off when the bombing had stopped.

My head felt bombarded with so much information. Why did it take a confrontation before my parents told us about the possibility of a war? Were they trying to protect us? How long could they protect us? As I think about it now maybe they felt the winds of war would not be severe; maybe it would just be a breeze and blow over. But what if the winds became a gale? There were more questions than answers and much uncertainty. My parents would later tell me that although they had prepared a war survival plan for the family, they wanted to protect us for as long as they could by not going into details earlier about the pending war.

My sisters and I shared a large room with five beds. The windows had mosquito proofing and were left open at night. My father said fresh air was the best air and "through and through" ventilation was the best in any room. Even so, we all slept under bed nets. As I reflect, it was actually like a boarding school room. We each had our corner with a little bedside cupboard. My mother would come in to say goodnight, tuck us in and turn off the lights. Once the lights were out there was to be no talking and we were meant to go to sleep. That night was different. None of us could sleep and we whispered into the late hours. With trepidation we imagined different scenarios. Some of my sisters felt everything had been fine until I came home with the story my friend had told me. I was not sure but I sort of felt they blamed me for disturbing their bliss. I know I was very inquisitive as a child. That night I felt like a TWW because of the speed with which I had passed on information about the pending war. My siblings and I coined the phrase TWW (Telephone Without Wires) for when information was passed at such speeds that phone wires or cables were not capable of, thus the information travelled through the air waves. This was long before the internet and broad band or wireless phones were invented. It seems that long before these wireless concepts, my siblings and I had unknowingly imagined that which was yet to be conceived. Maybe ignorance is truly bliss and I should not have passed on the information my friend told me.

My brothers snuck into our room to join in the discussion. They were not scared; they loved playing war games like Cowboys and Indians. This, however, was not a game. It was the threat of war, and war is real. Although I had never seen war, I was terrified. I did not sleep well that night. I had nightmares.

CHAPTER TWO

The war is upon us... The nation is asked to prepare

A FEW DAYS LATER, ON AN early July morning in 1967, we
woke up to soldiers marching in the rain and chanting war
songs. It looked as if they were training, but this was for
real. The moment had come. Civil war had started. The marching
became an early morning routine. We children would soon learn
one of the choruses whose words explicitly spelled out war:

> "We are the soldiers fighting for Nigeria,
> By the grace of Jesus we shall conquer."

I wondered why they were calling Jesus' name in reference to
the war. This was not Jesus' war. What did Jesus have to do with
it? I was used to calling and singing to Jesus at Anglican Sunday
school. I was not accustomed to his name being used by soldiers to
'conquer' in a war. Whose name was the other side going to use?
What if they called on God so they could conquer instead? Who
then would be victorious, God or Jesus? I was perplexed.

That morning, the radio announced that the war had started.
The eastern part of the country wanted to secede and establish
an independent country called Biafra. An army officer from the
East, Lt. Col Chukwuemeka Ojukwu, who was the commanding

federal military officer for the Eastern Region, was now leading the secessionist Biafran army. The Nigerian government's slogan became, **"To keep Nigeria one is a task that must be done."** A young good-looking northern officer named Yakubu Gowon, who was then Head of State, would lead the Nigerian side during the war. The spelling of his name, GOWON, became an acronym for **G**o **O**n **W**ith **O**ne **N**igeria!

Lt. Col. Ojukwu called upon all easterners to come home and join Biafra and help it gain liberation from Nigeria. The easterners left in droves, obeying his call and also fearing reprisal from the federal troops. As they arrived, young men were enlisted in the Biafran army. In response, Gowon declared the Biafran troops as Rebel forces, and took the battle to their home turf.

Lagos, the capital of the Federal Republic of Nigeria, was placed under high security. Checkpoints appeared on practically every road. Gun-toting federal soldiers with bloodshot eyes waved cars down screaming "Halt, who goes there? Stop to be *corcognized*." I later learned that what they meant to pronounce was actually "recognised." They would look into the car with piercing eyes and then laconically ask the driver to *"Open di boot"* or tell him *"Wetin de ya boot?"* I wondered what they were looking for. Surely people were not hiding in the boot. I was later told they were looking for bombs and ammunition.

I used to love going out, but now it was not so enticing. My mother was always calm when they stopped our car. She would hold our hands as she answered the soldiers' questions, reinforcing that we were her young children and she did not have any dangerous items in her car. She knew how not to antagonize them. She was brave and never seemed afraid of these fierce-looking soldiers. I felt safe with her.

I wondered what had happened that had led to hatred and division amongst the people. I did not quite grasp it then. Later as an adult, having listened to and read so many varied versions and interpretations of events that led to the civil war, I began to put together what caused the conflict that had such an impact on my life and destiny.

The fragile multiethnic, multireligious foundation on which Nigeria's independence was built by the British soon showed its cracks. At Independence the country was federated into three political units. The Northern Region consisted mainly of the Hausa, Fulani, Kanuri, Nupe and Tiv ethnic groups. The two southern regions were dominated in the West by the Yoruba and in the East by the Igbo. The Mid-Western Region, which included Benin my ancestral homeland, was a later addition. It was formed from ethnic minorities in the Western Region and consisted mainly of the Edo, Esan, Isekiri, Urhobo and Ijaw ethnic groups. The Ijaw also spanned across the creeks into other areas in the south eastern part of the country. Long before the colonial era these ethnic groups lived in rural villages separated from each other, developing their own dialects, languages and cultures.[1]

In addition to the religious, ethnic, linguistic and sociopolitical differences between the various regions, natural resources and wealth also varied. The West was rich in cocoa and palm oil, the East had coal and crude oil, the Midwest had timber, palm oil, crude oil and natural gas while the North had solid minerals, livestock and ground nuts. Each of the regions resented having to share its wealth with the ethnic groups in other parts of the country. Nor did the various ethnic groups feel much solidarity with most others. This

---

1 The main differentiator between ethnic groups is their dialect and to a lesser extent their culture. The origin of these differences could also have stemmed from their historical separateness. Take the Ijaw for example. Apart from their dialect, their separate history of coastal trade and coastal living with its ecological demands differentiates them as an ethnic group even though their geographical location spans across the Niger Delta. The Edo, and the Urhobo may have some cultural closeness but their different dialect and the unique history of the Edo people's great Benin Empire set them aside as different ethnic groups. The difference between the Hausa and Fulani stem from the latter's history of military conquest, migration and an imperial complex structure.

was not a great formula for building a unified nation, other than by force.

The amalgamation by the British of the Northern and Southern protectorates into a single country in 1914 without resolving the differences still haunted the country once Independence was achieved. Even before Independence, not every ethnic Nigerian agreed that freedom was desirable. The Kano Riots of May 1953 broke out as a result of the distrust and hostility between the Northerners and those Southerners who were pressing for Nigeria to become independent from colonial rule in 1956. The North was not so eager for an early independence. They felt disadvantaged not only in education but also politically and socioeconomically. If Nigeria became independent too early, they believed the South would rule them. As a result, Independence was delayed until 1960.

How deep-rooted and ancient these differences are was captured by Sylvia Leith-Ross in her book *Stepping Stones: Memoirs of Colonial Nigeria, 1907-1960*. Leith-Ross quotes a Hausa newspaper referring to hostilities between Hausa and Igbo

> Amongst some old papers, I found a cutting from the Hausa English newspaper *Gasikiya Ta Fi Kwabo* referring to the Commission of Enquiry into the Kano Riots (May 1953) ... when both Hausa and immigrant Ibo[2] lives were lost. A sentence [in the article] struck me: 'We were conquered by the white man but he did not enslave us and now those that did not conquer us seek to enslave us"

Leith-Ross then asked rhetorically, "There was self justification in [the observation]; did it also contain a threat?"

Nigeria held its first federal elections as an independent nation in 1964. Many said that the elections were greatly flawed, to

---

2   Ibo also referred to as Igbo in the book

the point of being fraudulent. All of the various political parties complained. The president, Dr. Nnamdi Azikiwe, found himself in a quandary. The Western Region elections in 1965 took political killings to a new level, and the rigged election results there were glaringly obvious. The rampant rioting, lawlessness and killings that followed were referred to as "Operation Wetie." People and property were drenched with gasoline and set ablaze, hence the term "Wetie." The government declared a state of emergency in the Western Region.

In January 1966, amid the political turmoil, chaos, confusion and corruption, the military staged a coup under the leadership of Major Chukwuma Patrick "Kaduna" Nzeogwu. He presented as a charming, young, determined man, who was dark in complexion and at times had a disarming smile. He looked every bit an officer and a gentleman. This first military coup is sometimes referred to as the January Coup, or Nzeogwu's Coup, because he made the foremost announcement of it. Due to the large number of majors who were involved, it is also known as the Majors' Coup. Nzeogwu and most of the majors involved were from the Eastern region.

Those killed in the coup were mainly Northerners of the Hausa and Fulani ethnic groups and included Prime Minister, Tafawa Balewa; Premier of the Northern Region, the Sarduana[3] of Sokoto, Ahmadu Bello; Brigadier Zakariya Maimalari, Lt Col. Abogo Largema (commander of 4th battalion), and Lt. Col. James Pam, who was the Adjutant General of the army. Non-northerners were also killed, including the commander of First Brigade, Brigadier Samuel Ademulegun; the Premier of the Western Region, Chief Ladoke Akintola; and the Federal Finance Minister, Chief Okotie Eboh, who was believed to be living a corrupt, flamboyant lifestyle. I believe the only Igbo military officer killed was Lt. Col Arthur Unegbe, who was the Quartermaster-General of the Federal

---

3   Sardauna is an influential traditional title in northern Nigeria

military. Unegbe's ethnicity is sometimes referred to as Mid-West Igbo. No Igbo politician was killed.

To the surprise of many, Nzeogwu's (or the Major's) coup was put down by the General Officer Commanding the Federal Nigerian Army, Major General Umunnakwe Aguyi Ironsi, who was a fellow Igbo. For the first time, Nigeria was under the rule of the armed forces. A Supreme Military Council headed by Ironsi was set up to exercise all political power. It immediately discharged the remaining members of the federal cabinet and replaced the elected premiers of the four regions with military governors. – Lt Col Chukwuemeka Odumegwu Ojukwu replaced Premier Michael Opara in the East; Lt. Col Francis Adekunle Fajuyi replaced assassinated Premier Ladoke Akintola in the West; Lt. Col Hassan Usman Katsina replaced assassinated Premier Ahmadu Bello in the North; and Lt Col. David Ejoor replaced Premier Denis Osadebe in the Mid-West.

Ironsi announced on May 24, 1966 that the Supreme Military Council had introduced Decree No. 34. The decree stated, amongst other things, that the former regions were abolished. Nigeria was reorganized into a number of territorial areas called provinces. A military governor subject to the direction and control of the head of the National Military Government was assigned to govern a group of provinces.

A few months later, in July 1966, officers mainly from the North led by Major Theophilus Y. Danjuma staged a countercoup. They felt their northern elders and senior officers had been targeted by mainly Igbo officers from the East in the earlier January coup. They were determined to avenge the deaths of their northern "brothers." General Ironsi was assassinated along with several senior and junior military officers from the East. The military governor of the Western Region, Lt. Colonel Fajuyi, who was hosting the visiting General Ironsi, was killed when he refused to hand him over to the coupists. Brigadier Babafemi Ogundipe, a southerner and the next

29

highest ranking officer, realizing he did not have the support of the northern military officers and could not control them, escaped to London. He would later accept a posting at the Nigerian High Commission in London. A northern Christian from Lur village in Plateau province in the middle belt of Nigeria, Colonel Yakubu Gowon, was chosen to become the head of state even though he was junior in the military hierarchy to Brigadier Ogundipe.

This time, the Igbo and some other groups felt their people had been deliberately targeted and killed during the Northern coup. Ethnic tension between the eastern Igbo and northern Hausa was especially severe. The chaos that ensued led to continued unauthorized, indiscriminate maiming and killing of Igbo people living in the north. Ojukwu asked all Igbo people to return to the East. They began to flee from the north and other parts of the country, heading back to their ancestral homelands. As they arrived in the East, the Igbo looked to Ojukwu to protect them.

In January 1967, the Nigerian military leadership went to Aburi, Ghana for a peace conference hosted by Gen. Joseph Ankrah, Ghanaian head of State and the army commander. Both Gowon and Ojukwu, who led the eastern delegates, were present. It was hoped that the Aburi Accord reached by both sides would resolve their hostilities.

However, ethnic suspicion, anxiety and mistrust remained at a high level. To ease tensions, a military decree was promulgated in May of 1967 that established twelve states to replace the four existing regions. Each of the states was to be governed by a military officer. The states were created to give the various ethnic groups more autonomy, especially the minorities who felt they were being subjected to intimidation in the Eastern Region. The states were also intended to undermine the larger administrative structures that gave regions their autonomy. The idea of a region seceding would thus be more difficult. It would also give the military a better control over the country.

In the May 1967 speech by Gowon declaring a twelve state structure for Nigeria, he stated:

> The country has a long history of well-articulated demands for states. ...I am satisfied that the creation of new states as the only possible basis for stability and equality is the overwhelming desire of vast majority of Nigerians. ... I must emphasize at once that the Decree will provide for a States Delimitation Commission which will ensure that any divisions or towns not satisfied with the states in which they are initially grouped will obtain redress.

Colonel Ojukwu, the military officer in charge of the Eastern Region, had become the main champion of the grievances of the Igbo, whose civilians had been the victims of pogroms in the North and whose military officers had been the main targets of the July 1966 coup. Ojukwu felt he had not been duly consulted on the creation of twelve states. The implementation of the agreements reached at Aburi soon became impossible. On May 30, 1967, Ojukwu declared that the Eastern Region was now the independent Republic of Biafra.

After attempts to dissuade Ojukwu failed, the Supreme Military Council resolved to act quickly against this declaration of secession, lest other parts of the Federation, especially the Western region, follow the East's example. Already there were rumours that the West would form the Oduduwa Republic if the East seceded. Thus, a year after the coup that installed Yakubu Gowon as head of state in 1966, the Nigerian Civil War began. The fate of the leader of the original coup, Nzeogwu, is still a matter of controversy. He survived the Northern coup but is believed to have been killed by

Federal troops in the East sometime in July 1967 at the beginning of the civil war. [4]

TIMELINE

1, October 1960

- Nigeria gains independence from British rule.

- Tafawa Balewa becomes Prime Minister, Nnamdi Azikiwe becomes President [5]

- Obafemi Awolowo is recognised as opposition leader.

1964- Nigeria's first election were held and President Azikiwe admitted they were flawed

1965- Western region elections marred by political killings – Operation Wetie

January 1966

- First military coup led by an Igbo, Major Nzeogwu. Northerners mainly killed including the prime minister Tafawa Balewa and northern premier Ahmadu Bello.

- Military rule introduced, Major General Aguyi Ironsi an Igbo took over as military leader.

July 1966

- Counter coup led by a northerner, Major T.Y Danjuma. Igbo mainly killed including military head of state Major General Aguyi Ironsi.

---

4   John de St. Jorre. The Brothers' war: Biafra and Nigeria (Houghton Mifflin Company Boston. 1972)

5   The Prime Minister was the leader of the government and the top political figure that had the power. The president was more of a ceremonial role.

- Col. Gowon, a northern Christian from Plateau State in the Middle Belt of Nigeria chosen to become Head of State.

- Hostilities break out between Igbo and Hausa resulting in the start of indiscriminate killing of Igbo in the north by Hausa.

- Col Ojukwu asks Igbo to return to the east.

January 1967
- Peace conference hosted by Ghanaian Head of State, Gen. Joseph Ankrah, to resolve hostilities between the east and north.

- Aburi Accord reached.

27, May 1967
- Gowon replaces the four regions of Nigeria with twelve states and assigns military governors to each state.

30, May 1967
- Col. Ojukwu declares eastern region an independent Republic of Biafra

July 1967
- Nigeria's head of State, General Gowon, insist on keeping Nigeria one nation declares Nigerian civil war.

Although a civil war was ongoing, my parents tried to maintain as much normalcy as possible. We still went to school during the week and church on Sunday. My siblings and I attended the Corona School, in Ikoyi. Most expatriates and civil servants sent their children there. The school was privately owned and charged fees. A mesh wire fence separated it from one of the better free government primary schools. There was a stark difference between the amenities in the two schools. Some of their teachers carried canes around. Beating students was permitted but not at Corona.

I often wondered why their school did not have the amenities mine had; why their teachers disciplined them with canes. We were all children so why should we have it so much better than they did? Some of my school mates and I would sometimes go to the fence and offer the children on the other side some of our lunch. They would generously offer us, in return, a popular fruit called "agbalumo" (African white star apple). Children loved "agbalumo" because, if the skin of the fruit was chewed long enough, it turned into chewing gum. Some of my friends and I would talk to them, trying to find out more about their school. Both schools later banned their students from talking across the fence. From an early age I thus began to realize, and question, the inequalities in life.

School days became tense after we students knew there was a war going on in our country. Few of us knew what war entailed. We were naturally frightened because we did not know what to expect. The senior students would gather together and pass on information their parents had either told them or they had overheard. The head mistress could feel the tension and fear in the air. She decided to address the issue at assembly. From what I remember, that morning we first sang an upbeat hymn. The head mistress played the piano beautifully as we all bellowed out the words. We said prayers and then everyone was asked to sit down. The headmistress briefly mentioned that the country was going through a war, but that we children should feel safe and not be afraid. It was important for us to listen to and obey our parents at home and teachers at school. During school hours, everything would be done to ensure our safety. To that end, rules and procedures had been put in place. During a bomb raid, teachers were to lead their classes to either the gym or assembly hall, depending on the grade. Everyone was to lie flat on the floor with their hands over their heads and their eyes closed. When the raids were over, sirens would signal that all was clear. Each teacher would take a roll call before heading back to their classroom. There another roll call would then be taken and parents who wanted to could collect their children early that day. These instructions would be posted clearly on notice boards throughout the school and sent to parents. From time to time there would be practice drills to determine how long it took to get everyone to their designated spots.

By now my siblings and I had resigned ourselves to the fact that there was a war going on. Our night watchman's name, Baba Beji, means "father of twins." He was fond of my younger siblings who were twins. Some evenings we would go to him on the verandah and ask him to tell us stories of his heroic battles in Burma during the Second World War. He would recount the details of his bravery at the front, but would reassure us that the civil war would not be like that. Since we were not in the war front, he told us, we had nothing to worry about.

The radio airwaves were full of information about the war and the fighting in the eastern part of the country. There were also public safety enlightenment announcements on the radio. One we loved listening to and knew by heart was...

> Stop careless talk, know what to do,
> Join the civil defense, it's for all of you.
> In case of a bomb attack, look out,
> Don't scream and shout.
> Don't run into the street broken glass will cut your feet.
> Don't look up into the sky flying objects may hit your eye,
> If in the market place fall flat on your face
> Do as you are told and you will live till you are old.

It went on with a list of dos and don'ts. The jingle had a really good beat. It's been several decades but I still remember it. In fact, the phrase "stop careless talk" became the mantra my younger siblings and I used whenever someone was saying something they should not be saying.

The battlefront was in the east. We lived in the west. War slowly began to seem less terrifying. It was not at our doorstep; nothing drastic had happened. A single night would change that.

Every night since the war began, before we went to bed, my parents would gather us together, say prayers, reassure us that the dawn would break just like it did every other day and we had nothing to fear. Yet one night, after midnight, (I remember because my father noted the time) the siren sounded for bomb raids. A loud bang jolted us all out of bed. My parents came to our room with a pen torchlight, lined us all up including my brothers in the adjacent room, did a quick head count and quickly led us in darkness to the space under the staircase. We lay flat, one beside another, each with our hands over our heads. I asked my mother what was going to happen to us if a bomb fell on our house. She told me not to worry, everything would be fine. It was as if she always knew, that she had a magic sense. Everything always turned out fine when she said it would, so I preferred asking her questions rather than my father when I needed reassurance.

That still dark night was shattered by moving bright lights from bombs exploding around us. It seemed like an eternity before the bombs stopped and the sirens finally sounded again that all was safe. We waited a few more minutes before we went back to our beds. My parents did another head count and we filed back to our bedrooms. Needless to say, no one slept a wink for the rest of the night. In the morning the radio announced that the Biafran army had sent mercenary fighters with planes to bomb the Dodan military barracks in southwest Ikoyi where General Yakubu Gowon, the head of state, resided. The bombers had missed their target and had hit a house in southwest Ikoyi instead. Luckily the family that lived in that house was away, so no one got killed. Other bombs had landed in an open field inside the barracks' perimeter. The bomber plane had been shot down and the pilots had died.

My parents took us to see the bombed house, which was located less than fifteen minutes from where we lived and open for public viewing. It felt like visiting a museum as people walked around slowly taking in everything. There was a big hole in the roof and in the ceiling. Shattered glass was scattered everywhere and the sidewall had crumbled. Part of the bomb had actually landed on the couple's bed and had been left there for viewing. I began to wonder if this was what people in the war front or war zones were facing. As for me, I just wanted the war to end. I wanted to feel safe again. The war that had seemed so far away suddenly felt so chillingly near.

Soon after that day, my Palestinian friend told me at school that her parents said they were leaving Nigeria because of the war. She was not sure when they were leaving, but she would have a party for her friends before she left. Since I was one of her closest friends she wanted me to make sure I would be there. I promised her I would not miss it. Unfortunately, I would later break that promise due to no fault of mine.

CHAPTER THREE

Compulsory vacation...Benin, my native land

MY FAMILY USUALLY TRAVELLED TO Benin City[6] during Christmas vacation or summer vacations. My Palestinian friend had set a date for her combined birthday and farewell party. I had told her I would be there and I intended to keep my promise. My father and his younger brother, who lived up the road from us with his family, had decided both families should go to Benin for the holidays because it would be safer for us children to be away from Lagos. As soon as school vacation started, we would drive to Benin in a convoy. When I heard this, I begged my parents to delay the trip by a day. My friend was leaving for good and I so wanted to go to the party. She was one of my closest friends and she needed me there. I was very sad and annoyed when my parents said we could not postpone the trip and that I had to bid her farewell on the last day of school before the holidays.

Benin was about a six-hour road trip, and involved careful preparations. The drivers had to make sure the cars were in good

---

6   Benin City is the capital of Edo State in Southern Nigeria. It was the center of the former great Benin Empire whose influence was vast and extended west through the country of Dahomey whose name was changed to Republic of Benin in 1975 after the Bight of Benin, the body of water on which it lies. It is situated in West Africa and shares a border with Nigeria.

condition, fill the tanks with fuel and check the tire pressures. The nannies had to prepare snacks we would eat on the way. We children had to pack our clothes and things we would need over the vacation. We were not allowed to pack too many things individually because we had only two suitcases between us all. We were usually excited when we were going on such a journey, but this time we were apprehensive.

The ancient city of Benin was the capital of the newly created Midwest State, which geographically served as a buffer between the west and the east of Nigeria. It was the ancestral home of both my parents. My mother was a descendant of King Ovonramwen, who was on the throne during the British invasion of the Benin Empire in 1897. He was later deposed by the British and sent into exile in Calabar.[7] Her grandfather, Agho Obaseki, and father, Gaius Ikuobase Obaseki had been the head of all chiefs or the prime minister of the Edo, otherwise known traditionally as the Iyase of Benin. Her grandmother Princess Edugie, was bestowed on her grandfather by King Ovonramwen.

My parents instilled in us their pride in their Benin heritage and language, Edo. They taught us the glorious history of the Benin Empire and our rich cultural legacy exemplified by the world-renowned sculptures called Benin Bronzes[8].

My mother was a princess, and I was a descendant of King Ovonramwen. She was part of a large, extended family. My mother

---

7   Calabar is a city in Cross-River State in South-East Nigeria. It is to the east of Benin and lies along the Calabar River. It was an important shipping port and a center of trade for European traders. Calabar was under British protection in 1897 when Oba Ovoranwen was sent to exile. He died in Calabar and is buried there.

8   Benin Bronzes are art sculptures and plaques made from bronze or brass alloys by the guild of bronze casters using the lost wax method. The most famous are the ones made between the fifteenth and eighteenth century, looted from the Oba's palace during the British invasion and are now in the British and other western museums. So renowned are they that Museum of Fine Arts Boston built a special gallery for them.

had several siblings with whom she shared the same father, but not mother, and one sibling, her sister, with whom she shared the same mother but not father. She was the only surviving child her parents had together. She often talked about her full brother Dominick, who was poisoned to death as a little boy. She said her mother believed he was poisoned because he was the eldest son and would become the primary heir to all her father's vast fortunes. Being the mother of the eldest male child was a status highly coveted by the wives in a polygamous setting. It was a powerful position to have. My mother said the death of her brother Dominick left my grandmother so devastated that she could not bear to remain in my grandfather's compound, where her son had been poisoned. After my grandmother left, my mother was cared for in the compound by her grandmother Princess Edugie. My grandmother remained brokenhearted over the death of her son and fondly talked about him to me, even though I was a child.

The journey to Benin began at about seven in the morning. My uncle arrived with his family, all packed into one car. There were no seat belts in those days and you could easily put five children in the back. My father, on the other hand, believed in separating the family and never put us all in the same car or plane when we traveled. That morning we would make the journey in two cars. My mother's was a white Opel Kapitän. My younger siblings always traveled with her. They were twins and the last born children. She called them her babies. Most of my siblings loved traveling with her. The trip was fun in her car because she packed lots of cookies and drinks; you could eat, sleep and talk as much as you wanted. It was always full of laughter.

My mother had never learned how to drive so she always had to put her trust in her driver, Taiwo, a middle-aged family man. He was a twin. My mother, having given birth to twins, had a soft spot for them. Taiwo's wife and two children lived on our compound. My mother felt a man with a family would be a more responsible driver and she could trust him to drive her children because he would always want to return to his family. Taiwo had been our driver for as long as I can remember and was a very good and caring one. Somehow I don't remember my father's driver's name or his car in the 1960s. I do however remember that he was stern but nice, and very professional.

My father liked me travelling in his car, and I enjoyed it and found it quite stimulating. I could never sleep when riding in a car and my father believed you should never fall asleep whilst you are being driven. You had to keep watch so the driver did not doze off. He would make us count all the bridges we crossed; discuss the different types of vegetation we passed; learn how the roads were made and the materials that were used such as granite, laterite, and tar. He used every opportunity to educate and enlighten us. He was a big believer in education and was knowledgeable in many fields.

My father's car always led the way. My mother's car followed. My uncle drove behind her as we moved in a three-car convoy. The journey lasted ten hours rather than the usual six. There were no dual carriageways and we went from town to town along narrow roads, avoiding the main roads because of the war. Even on the secondary roads we passed through a lot of checkpoints. We also passed a convoy of military tankers, or rather, they passed us. My father tried to put on the radio to find out whether something was happening, but he could not get a signal from the main stations.

Whenever we traveled to Benin before the war, we would stop on the way and have a picnic. Other families did that too. The roads were safe; there were no armed robbers or bandits. Our favorite spot was the town of Ore, which had lots of local restaurants that made food the old fashioned way in earthenware pots with fresh herbs and natural ingredients. The restaurants were basically mud huts with thatched roofs. The décor consisted of low benches and tables. The menu was filled with native delicacies such as large snails, cow legs, goat head pepper soup, fish head pepper soup, *Ewedu* (a draw soup made of diced green leaves and crayfish), *Amala* (yam flour made with hot water into a starchy consistency), pounded yam, okra stew, *Edikang ikong* soup (multi vegetable leaf and periwinkle soup), *Ogbono* (a draw soup made from ground African mango seed and crayfish), *Eba* (cassava flour made with hot water into a dense consistency), and *Dundun* (big chunks of yam coated and deep fried in palm oil). Our drivers loved to eat in Ore but my father would not let us eat there because he felt the restaurants were not hygienic enough. I think I inherited my obsessive hygiene traits from my father.

That day, however, we would not be stopping anywhere. We would all eat in our cars as we drove along. It was too dangerous to stop. I remember only a brief stop that was made at a petrol station to top up the fuel tanks and so everyone could use the restroom. There were too many military tankers with fierce looking soldiers on the road. We were moving very slowly and staying out of their way. My father seemed on edge throughout the trip. He felt great responsibility for his family. I even heard him mutter to the driver once that it may not have been a good day to travel as more military tankers drove by. We could not turn back, however. We were two thirds of the way, almost at Ore. I had mixed emotions when I heard my father say that. I felt cross because I remembered I was missing my friend's party. I also felt worried and wished I was traveling in my mother's car.

My mother always acted as if everything was fine, even when it was not. My mother's phrase was always "everything will be fine," even when it looked as if it wouldn't be. My father, on the other hand, believed in always critically analyzing things. My mother did not believe in overanalyzing. They were the yin and the yang, yet they loved and fitted each other. They remained married for over forty years till my father died.

We finally got to Benin in the evening. Whenever we arrived in Benin we would drive to my mother's sister's house to inform her we had arrived. We would then go on to my parents' country home in New Benin. My mother's sister lived in a house my mother had inherited from her father. My grandmother also lived there and my aunt cared for her. When we arrived, we found a large crowd of aunts and uncles gathered in my aunt's house. When they heard our cars pull up and the horns blow, which was our usual signal that we had arrived, there was shouting and jubilation. They all ran out, hugging and kissing us. I wondered what was going on. They said they had heard rumours that the Biafran troops and the Federal troops were involved in a serious gun battle as the Biafran troops were advancing. They were not sure what route we had taken and were afraid we may have been caught in the crossfire. In those days there were no cell phones, no Blackberry messengers, no high tech gadgets and very few landlines phones. Once you were on the road, you were incommunicado. The adults went into a room to talk. My aunt took us in and fed us. My granny came out of her room, hugged all of us one by one and thanked God we had arrived safely. We were very close and when she prayed for me she seemed to take extra time.

Granny had the smoothest, silkiest skin I had ever seen. She had no wrinkles and a twinkle in her eye. She was always neatly dressed and had a tobacco pipe she smoked. It was fashionable for elderly people to smoke pipes in the 1960s. Above all, Granny had an unforgettable smile and laugh.

They must have fed the adults in a separate room because when we finished eating my parents bundled us into the car and we went to our country home. My uncle took his family, to their home, which was located in a different part of town.

That night I lay in my bed in Benin City pondering the day's events. The gun battle must have been why we saw all those army tankers. If only my parents had stayed the extra day in Lagos we would have found out about the advancing Biafran soldiers.

CHAPTER FOUR

Invasion...Biafran soldiers reach Benin

WE WERE AWAKENED AT SIX a.m. by the sound of mortars fired into the city. My parents had managed to make a few phone calls to find out what was happening in the center of town before Biafran troops cut off all telecommunications. The few landlines that existed had been disconnected. I remember our phone number was just three digits - 110. In those days, people were not dependent on phones. In fact, most people did not have one, and information was primarily passed on by word of mouth.

I looked out of the living room window. The streets were deserted, apart from lorry loads of fierce looking Biafran soldiers carrying guns and chanting war songs. They were trying to root out any Federal soldiers who had gone into hiding. Apparently, when the Federal soldiers realized that they had been overpowered, some took off their uniforms and fled the barracks in civilian clothing.

As always, my mother tried to remain calm and reassuring. She went to the kitchen and began to make our favorite breakfast, which consisted of Heinz baked beans in tomato sauce, omelets and sausages. Usually, the morning after we arrived in Benin, my aunt would cook a traditional Nigerian breakfast consisting of fried yams, boiled plantains, *moyin-moyin* (steamed bean cakes), *akara* (fried bean cakes), pap, tomato stew with assorted meat and a palm oil stew called *owo*. She would bring it to our house early in the morning as a welcome breakfast, since we had just arrived and were probably still exhausted from the trip. That morning however, there would be no aunt bringing breakfast because there was no movement in Benin. The city was under siege.

My aunt was very good at cooking traditional dishes and I loved the wholesome taste of her food. My mother was good at preparing both traditional and western food and I loved her cooking as well. I learned how to cook from her. Nigerian mothers (and mothers in virtually every other nation) trained their daughters to cook in those days. Food was prepared fresh daily. There were no microwaves, no frozen packet foods, and no fast food joints. People took the time to cook; they took the time to do things. When breakfast was ready and laid out on the table, my mother called us all to the dining room. My older sisters had been helping her in the kitchen. I had been told to stop looking out of the window and was back in my bedroom thinking of all my friends I had left in Lagos, my school, our home, and when I would see them again. I opened the door of my room and walked into the dining room, a long corridor that opened out onto a veranda. I believe the space had been converted because we had an especially long dining room table to fit all of us. The veranda overlooked the backyard, which was a narrow strip of land consisting of typical Benin red soil and a very high brick wall.

The radio was on in the background as we ate breakfast. My mother smiled and kept putting more food out. This was one morning we were allowed to have as many helpings as we wanted. My father spent most of the time tuning the hand held transistor radio. He was trying to tune to the BBC (British Broadcasting Corporation) or VOA (Voice of America). The BBC, I later learned, had the best coverage throughout the Nigerian civil war, also referred to as the Biafran war. He finally tuned into the BBC. The station gave a complete account of what had happened in the battle that led to the Biafran soldiers invading Benin.

I remember my father started to explain to us the implication of what had just been broadcast and how it affected us as a family. The two things I remember from that conversation were that we were stuck in Benin indefinitely, and that Benin was now part of Biafra. I reminded my father, that if only we had waited in Lagos a day longer so I could attend my friend's party, we would not have been caught up in the war. He did not react angrily to my childish complaint. As usual, I then began to ask all the questions. What about school? How would we go to school? Were we now Biafrans, because I wanted to remain a Nigerian? Back in Lagos, the Federal government said the Biafrans were rebels but the Biafrans said they were liberators fighting for self-determination. Who was right? My mother intervened and told me not to worry. Everything would be fine.

Nonetheless, my parents told us to keep the windows shut and stay indoors. We were not allowed to play in the front garden of our home in Benin, a bungalow with a large garden in front planted with fruit trees and flowers that in the evenings was lit up by fluorescent lights. The bungalow had two garages attached to the side of the house. Our caretaker lived with his family in the quarters beside the house. My father told him to make sure he kept the garden lights off so the house would not attract attention. He also instructed him that the gate leading to the house, which was usually open, should now be kept locked.

In the past, whenever we returned to Benin, our gates were usually flung open and our house was a mecca that attracted uncles, aunts and cousins. My parents were relatively well off. My mother's father had been a timber magnate who exported lumber to England and owned a lot of land. My mother had inherited some of his wealth when he died. Our visits home gave the extended family an opportunity to visit, and for those in need to put forward their requests for assistance. As a result, my parents were pleased to pay school fees for our cousins, or to give our aunts seed money to start a business.

My father, on the other hand, grew up an orphan. When he was very young, his mother died tragically during childbirth from obstructed labour. She and her stillborn twins were buried together. His father, who had been converted to Christianity by the missionaries and was a preacher, took only one wife despite the traditional custom of polygamy. He loved her deeply and died shortly after her from a broken heart. Despite his situation, my father was determined to get an education. He was an excellent student and was able to get scholarships all the way through, eventually even to study in England. He had trained as an engineer, joined the Nigerian colonial civil service and rose by merit to the top.

By the time I was born, my family was upper middle class. In the 1960s that meant I experienced a very comfortable upbringing compared to the average Nigerian. We enjoyed summer vacations in England, cruises on the ships *Elder Dempster* and *MV Aureol*. Nonetheless, my parents taught us to share our bounty with our large extended family. They also made sure we were not spoilt and my mother ensured that we were not dependent on the helps but assisted with all domestic chores. She also stressed to us the importance of personal service to the community. My mother was a great believer in social justice.

At that moment, however, everything seemed very uncertain. I went to the bathroom after breakfast and wept as I thought of the friend I may never see again. She would know what to do if she were around. She knew about wars and what happened to children caught up in them. After all, if not for her I would never have known about the war when I did. I loved Lagos; I wanted to be there; and I wanted to be a Nigerian. That was who I was. I had broken my promise: I had missed her farewell party, and maybe that was why I was caught up in warfare. Dawn quickly became dusk. There was a dusk to dawn curfew. Since our house was a bungalow, there was no staircase and no space underneath which we could take shelter if there were air raids. This time, my father said we should take shelter underneath our beds.

Sporadic gunshots rang out throughout the night. By nine o'clock the next morning, the advancing Biafran rebel army had captured Benin and the entire Mid-West. They were led by Lt Col. Victor Banjo and got as far as Ore, which is less than two hundred miles from Lagos. Although he was a Yoruba, Victor Banjo had aligned himself with Biafra. Earlier, he felt he had been unjustly accused of participating in a coup against the Federal government and had been imprisoned in the East. Ojukwu set him free at the beginning of the war to liberate Biafra from the federation, and Banjo felt a loyalty and bond to Ojukwu. It was also rumoured that Banjo intended to liberate the West from the federation as well.

Some Benin people held the erroneous assumption that "all Igbo were rebels." It was believed by some that the Biafran rebels wanted to take the Mid-West because it was the only oil producing area in Nigeria, other than the South-East, which they already controlled. It was also a strategic gateway between the east and the west. Capturing it would cripple the economy of the rest of the country. Many non-Igbo also believed that the Biafran troops were able to capture Benin so easily because the resistance from the mid-western Igbo who were part of the Federal army was insincere. As a result, the non-Igbo citizens of Benin began to mistrust the mid-western Igbo as much as they mistrusted their Igbo neighbours.

By noon the rebels had rooted out and killed most of the Federal soldiers who had been in hiding, and felt they were in firm control. Their commander made an announcement welcoming Benin into Biafra. We were told that it was now a crime to hide any Federal soldiers or northerners in general. If we knew where they were hiding, we should report them to the new authorities. Otherwise, they encouraged people to go about their normal business, but to observe the curfew.

My father's cousin lived a couple of houses away on the same street. He had also come to Benin for the holidays. His family lived in Benin, although he worked in another city. His son spent a lot of time gathering information by visiting local bars and going from house to house to chat with local residents. We nicknamed him "the informant." He even made friends with the Biafran soldiers. Whenever my father's cousin's son came around, my mother would make sure he ate a big meal as we gathered to listen to his stories. At times, they seemed far-fetched, but he made us laugh by listening to him. His speech was occasionally slurred and one could easily pass him off as not knowing what he was saying, but it turned out that much of the time he did. He later became a very useful informant during our period of captivity, managing to get information from his soldier friends and then coming to tell us what was going on.

After a week, the people of Benin City began to live a cautious existence despite rebel rule. It was not uncommon to find bullet casings on the ground. Although the market women kept their stalls open, food was becoming scarce because people were stockpiling and few villagers were braving the journey into the city to sell their goods.

CHAPTER FIVE

God save our King... Where is the Oba of Benin?

IN THE SIXTIES, BENIN WAS still steeped in its traditions and its reverence for the King, who was called the Oba. "Oba ghator okpere" ("Long live the king") his subjects would proclaim in Edo at the end of their sentences whenever they referred to him. Their prayers, when uttered in the native dialect, would usually conclude with the same incantation. The Oba was the symbol of their unity and the embodiment of their tradition. There was a mutual love and a sacred relationship between the people and the king, who they saw as their spiritual leader.

As with most royal rulers throughout history, it was considered heretical and sacrilegious to speak evil of the Oba. His prerogatives were not to be challenged. Family names actually spelt out the Edo peoples' beliefs about their Oba. For example the name Aiguobasimwin means one does not tussle with the King for anything; Aitortorobahor - one does not speak evil of the King; Aiseokhuoba - one should not attract the wrath, war or curse of the King. The traditional belief was that whoever betrayed the King would be cursed. A feared traditional Edo curse "Oba gha gbue" means "the king will kill you."

People believed that the Oba had mystical powers and was in communication with his ancestors. The oracles were consulted daily. Even though Benin had a democratic, parliamentary system of government during the first political dispensation,[9] the people still saw themselves as subjects of the Oba. The Oba reigned but did not rule. The Oba did not eat in public. He only received or attended to visitors at certain times of the year and had to perform many traditional rituals to ensure that his subjects and kingdom were kept safe. Through changing times, the king was a constant figure that was honoured, respected, feared and loved. He was believed to be imbued with the virtues of courage and justice. Traditional matters were decided by him and the Oba's word was the last word…the King spoke, and it was so. The Oba's traditional council of chiefs had various titles and was headed by the Iyase of Benin. A woman could not become a chief for traditional reasons relating to her anatomy. It was an abomination for a woman to perform any rituals or enter into a shrine during certain times of her menstrual cycle.

In the ancient Kingdom of Benin, the Oba was the focal point of social cohesion. The families belonged to different guilds which were all under his commission. There was a social order that allowed talent to flourish. Benin people took pride in their heritage. The world-famous Benin bronzes, confiscated, now on display in the British Museum in London were made by casters belonging to the Bronze Guild. Children either learned in school or through oral history about the British invasion of the Benin Empire in 1897, also referred to as "the punitive expedition." This invasion led to thousands of bronzes and other precious works of art being taken from the Oba's palace by the British soldiers, after which the palace was burnt down and the King sent into exile.

Basil Davidson cites Dutch accounts of the splendour of the Empire and the grandeur of the King's palace.

---

9   The first political dispensation, also referred to as the First Republic, was the period of government in Nigeria starting at independence from colonial rule till the first military coup on January 15th 1966.

Being commercially and technically more advanced than other Europeans of the 17th century, the Dutch were better reporters. In 1668, the Dutchman Olfert Dapper published his immediately famous description of Africa containing a number of invaluable reports on the condition of Benin. According to these reports, 'The empire by that time according to these witnesses measured some four hundred and fifty miles from West to East and unknown distances towards the north having many towns and infinity of villages, the capital itself being enclosed on one side by the wall ten feet high made of a double palisade of trees pierced by several gates eight or nine feet high and five feet wide each made of a single piece of wood and turning on a stake.

The king's palace, these Hollanders reported, is on the right side of the town...being a collection of buildings which occupy as much space as the town of Harlem, with numerous apartments and fine galleries most of which are as big as those on the exchange in Amsterdam. These galleries were supported by wooden pillars encased with copper where their victories were depicted...while the corner of each gallery roof is adorned with a small pyramidal tower, on the point of which is perched a copper bird spreading its wings. The whole town is composed of thirty main streets, very straight and 120 feet wide apart from an infinity of small intersecting streets, the houses being closer to one another arranged in good order and these people are in no way inferior to the Dutch as regards cleanliness', no mean tribute from the members of a nation that was probably in point of cleanliness, the most advanced in Europe of its day.[10]

I learned about the British invasion both in school and from my ancestors. Both my parents had told me the story and I have since passed it on to my daughter. My mother often recited the chronicle of the invasion with particular passion because she was a descendant of the King on the throne, Oba Ovonramwen.[11] Plays of great historical and theatrical value have been written about the punitive invasion during his reign.

Benin was once a mighty empire with an advanced level of development, complex social structures and organizations, material and artistic progress. When the Portuguese and Dutch arrived in the 17th century, they were impressed by its wealth, strength, and splendour. They found it a neat and well planned city. In reference to the Benin Empire, Portuguese Captain, Lourenco Pinto noted:

> Great Benin where the king resides is larger than Lisbon, all the streets runs (sic) straight as far as the eye can. The houses are large, especially that of the king which is richly decorated and has five columns. The city is wealthy and industrious. It is so well governed that theft is unknown and the people live in such security. The artisans have their places carefully allocated in the squares which are divided up in such a manner that in one square I counted altogether one hundred and twenty smiths workshops all working continuously."[12]

---

10 Basil Davidson, *The African Past* (London: Longman, 1964), p. 183.

11 His full title was Oba Ovonramwen Nogbaisi (crowned in 1888- died in 1914).

12 Footnote 3, Page 113 Benin and the Europeans by Prof A.F.C. Ryder published by Longmans 1969

Benin City was protected by a man-made moat that was a marvel to the outside world. This moat is now listed as a national monument. Referring to the Benin moat, Fred Pearce wrote:

> They extend for some 16,000 kilometres in all, in a mosaic of more than 500 interconnected settlement boundaries. They cover 6,500 square kilometres and were all dug by the Edo people. In all, they are four times longer than the Great Wall of China, and consumed a hundred times more material than the Great Pyramid of Cheops. They took an estimated 150 million hours of digging to construct, and are perhaps the largest single archaeological phenomenon on the planet.[13]

The Benin Empire was a very guarded society, steeped in traditional rituals. During some of these rituals the city was closed to foreigners and the King received no guests. My great grandfather, Chief Agho Obaseki, was given the Obaseki chieftaincy title by King Ovonramwen. He also later became the Iyase of Benin, leader of the King's advisory council, during the reign of King Eweka II. He was Ovonramwen's best friend and son-in-law. They had been friends since childhood and Agho was the Oba's most trusted confidant. The King had betrothed Princess Edugie, to him. She and Agho had two children together, a son named Gaius who was my grandfather and a daughter named Eronmwon. Gaius like his father also later became the Iyase of Benin. Although Agho was an important palace chief and the King's right hand man, they did not see eye to eye on a number of things. Agho was an astute business man and believed that Benin's borders should be open for trade. Even though the Dutch and Portuguese were already trading with Benin, the King remained skeptical and resisted further opening

---

13   Pearce, Fred. *African Queen*. New Scientist, 11 September 1999, Issue 2203.

up of the kingdom to other countries. He feared things could get out of control if his subjects were exposed to too many outside influences and dangers.

England's Queen Victoria had received reports of a great kingdom in Africa called the Benin Empire. She sent a small contingent of British soldiers on an expedition with a message of greeting to its King. Unfortunately, they arrived at a time when the palace was going through a period of important rituals and outsiders were not welcome. When the King was informed of the arrival of the British messengers, he called his council of chiefs together. My great grandfather Agho Obaseki, as the trusted confidant of the king and a senior member of the council of chiefs, was amongst those at the meeting. When all the chiefs had gathered round, the King explained the dilemma to them. The Queen of England had sent out emissaries to greet him, but he could not receive them because of the traditional ceremonies and rituals going on at the palace during which the entry or welcoming of foreigners into the kingdom was forbidden. However, he did not want to be rude and send the English travelers back without giving them an audience.

Some of the chiefs felt the King should not receive them at all and others felt he should. My great-grandfather Agho believed it would be wrong to send them back without hearing what message they brought. He saw it as an opportunity for Benin to become exposed to England and beyond, but he was also mindful of the importance of adhering to tradition and of not offending the gods. The soothsayers consulted their oracle and were very worried by what they saw. They felt there was an imminent disaster associated with the visit and said the King should not offend the gods by allowing the Queen of England's soldiers in during the forbidden period. The king, after much consultation, said he would see them but they would have to wait on the outskirts of Benin until a time when foreigners would be allowed to enter the kingdom. He said that if they could not wait they should come back at another time and convey his good wishes to the Queen. He sent some of his chiefs to deliver this message to them.

Unbeknownst to the King, the chiefs he sent took it upon themselves to decide that they would not allow these British soldiers ever to enter Benin. On arriving at the site where the British soldiers were located, the chiefs ambushed and killed all of them, or so they thought. However, two soldiers managed to escape and reported back to Queen Victoria that the emissary she sent had been savagely killed. The Queen decided to send a fleet of soldiers on a punitive expedition to Benin. To the surprise and shock of the King, the British invaded his empire in 1897. He only learned later what his disobedient chiefs had done. It was too late; the British had come for revenge. The King was captured, put on the British Niger Coast Protectorate yacht *SY Ivy*, and sent east of Benin, down the Calabar River into exile in Calabar,[14] never to return to his subjects.

The British burnt down his palace after pilfering from it thousands of ancient Benin bronzes and other priceless works of art. The stolen booty was sent to England and presented to the Queen. The Bronzes are today, along with the plundered Elgin Marbles, the jewels in the crown of the artistic holdings of the British Museum. Other parts of Benin City were burnt down or destroyed and several inhabitants were killed. The Benin people became subjects of the Queen of England; the Union Jack waved above them. The Benin Empire was no more. Its King transitioned to be with his ancestors in lonely exile seventeen years later in 1914, the year his British enemies embarked upon a far greater military venture – The First World War.

The Benin dynasty was restored in 1914 after the King's passing. His son returned to Benin City and was crowned Oba Eweka II. Benin has never forgotten its dark period when the British invaded, plundered their precious bronzes, and their King was banished to exile in Calabar. The people vowed such humiliation should never again be meted on their King. The people woke up every morning,

---

14 Calabar a coastal city which was under British protection later became part of southeastern Nigeria and is currently situated in Cross-River State.

prayed for him and awaited eagerly for messages about his well-being from the palace town criers and messengers.

In 1967, when the Biafrans invaded Benin, King Akenzua II[15] was on the throne. He was a dark, slim, educated man. He attended Kings College Lagos, the premier boy's college. He was seen in public in the splendour of his whole traditional attire only during certain traditional functions or special events. This attire usually consisted of white outfits with a large assortment of coral beads on the body and head. During certain other periods and rituals the King wore red. He was beloved and communicated well with the people through his chiefs and town criers. The marketplace was where information was commonly disseminated. One of the major market places was called Eki Oba, which means the King's market.

After the Biafran invasion on August 9, 1967, information from the palace suddenly came to a halt. Although the markets were initially closed, people expected that news about the King would still filter to the people. Wild rumours began to abound. One was that the King had turned into a fly on the wall and when the Biafran soldiers came into the palace he escaped by flying away. The people believed their King possessed such mystical powers. Another rumour was that the King had actually been captured and placed incommunicado so he would not instigate the people to revolt. The King's name was said to be on the list of those to be executed at a later date. The rumours were spreading like wildfire; the people were not only worried for themselves but also for their King. People began to whisper amongst themselves, asking 'Where is the King?' Soothsayers were consulting their gods to ascertain the whereabouts of the King. Everyone was also praying fervently ... "Oba ghator okpere" ... "Long live the King" ... "God save our King."

---

15   His full title was Akenzua N'iso N'orro II (reigned from 1933-1979 CE).

CHAPTER SIX

The Executioners' List: "Run for your life"

RUMOUR SPREADS FOR SO MANY reasons. These include uncertainties, fear, lack of information, misinformation, partial information or leaked information. Whatever the reason is, when the rumours start they spread like wildfire, and depending on the rumours and the circumstances, they can lead to pandemonium.

Benin had been captured by the Biafrans. Conditions that breed rumour mongering were very ripe. During the war, gossip would start from leaked information. It could start off contained, but by the time it got to places where people gather such as the market, church or mosque it would take on a multiplier effect. During captivity, trying to guess the captors' next move was like playing a game of chess. Top secrets of officials are usually guarded from everyone except those they do not perceive as a threat: their drivers, domestic staff, the market women, labourers and children they encounter. Yet, these very people are often the first source of rumours.

The village women brought in their goods from their farms in wooden trucks called "mammy wagons." Some of these trucks were similar to the covered wagons drawn by horses in cowboy movies. Now, the trucks had engines in front. They were crudely fashioned with a bench for the driver that usually held two other passengers as well. The wagons were decorated with inscriptions - either a verse from a psalm, a proverb or a saying. A favorite was from the 23rd Psalm: "The Lord is my shepherd." The drivers figured it was consoling to know that He was guiding them on their journey. Another popular inscription was "Let them say." How I loved that one. The adage was telling people to get on with their lives and stop worrying excessively about what others said about them – ignore the opinions of the crowd and do what you think is right.

The back of the wagon was open space for carrying goods. If the driver wanted to take passengers instead, he would put in removable benches. Travelers would climb into the back with the help of a stool. In Benin, back in the sixties, there were no vehicle or passenger safety regulations or enforcement.

At the crack of dawn, the village women would load their goods onto the mammy wagons and head to the city markets, where they sold them to the market women. The three main markets I remember then were "Eki Oba" which means the King's market; Eki Agbado, or Communal Market, in which we all trade together; and Garage market, also called New Benin market. Garage was a makeshift market that had started at a motor park site to cater to the growing number of people moving to the New Benin area on the outskirts of the city center. Garage Market was nearest to our house and the one at which my mother most often shopped. Eki Agbado was the nearest market to where my grandmother lived. The Oba's market was located in the center of the city. Each market had its market day that varied from week to week.

Every market woman craved to have a stall or space for her goods at Oba's market. It had a shrine built in honour of Emotan, a 15th-century market woman famous for her bravery and loyalty to Prince Ogun, who later became Oba Ewuare I, the 12th Oba of Benin. Emotan was responsible for saving the King and ensuring that the Benin Royal line of accession was adhered to. By tradition, the line of royal succession in Benin Kingdom goes to the eldest male child. For a period of time, Oba Uwaifiokun the younger brother of Prince Ogun, had exiled him and ascended the throne in his place (1430AD-1440AD). Emotan became friendly with Prince Ogun during his exile and would shelter him when he secretly visited Benin. She would counsel him and pass on whatever information she had gathered regarding those chiefs loyal to his younger brother. When he eventually ascended the throne as Oba Ewuare, Ogun did not forget Emotan's good deeds. After her death, he declared the spot where she had traded her goods at Oba's market a sacred shrine, and that the Uruhe tree be planted there. From that day forth he ordered that every coronation of a king in Benin must include paying homage to the Emotan shrine. Locals visited the memorial, performed sacrifices and made their prayer requests.

Still today, homage is paid there by natives whenever they are performing traditional ceremonies. In 1954, a life- size bronze statue of Emotan dressed in Benin traditional attire replaced the shrine's tree. The statue was unveiled by Oba Akenzua II, who was still on the throne in 1967 when the Biafrans invaded and captured Benin.

Despite Benin being under captivity, the Oba's market was a beehive of activity. It was also a good place for information gathering. Everyone needs food to survive, so the market was a place that they had to visit frequently. This made the marketplace the center of rumour mongering. One rumour that would not go away was about a list that had been prepared by the Biafran soldiers. Market women, traders and craftsmen felt they were no threat, so their names would not be on the list. Top civil servants, industrialist and business men, however, felt differently. The non-Igbo civil servants were especially vulnerable. They were the engines that efficiently ran the Nigerian federal ministries.

The rumours intensified about what soon became referred to as the "executioner's list," eventually reaching frightening dimensions for my family. There were false reports that some on the list had been selected for secret execution. The market women were so shocked that they began to warn their regular customers whose husbands they perceived might be in danger due to the positions they held. My mother came home from the market one day and informed my father that she had been told his name was on the list and he was in danger.

My parents' cars were locked up in our two-car garage, which was built so the spaces were separate units. My mother's Opel Kapitän was parked on the inner side nearer the house, my father's on the outside. The two large wooden doors were kept closed and secured with huge padlocks. The garages were not locked for the safety of the cars, but to give the impression that the owners of the house were out of town. Our automobiles had out of town license plates that my father felt would immediately give our identity away as people who lived in the capital city Lagos and, thus, most probably worked for the civil service. The batteries and the vehicles were locked up. An uncle brought my father an inconspicuous looking car with local plates whenever my parents needed to go out. My father avoided going out as much as possible. Now that the news had been received that most likely his name was on the list of those to be executed, my parents' extended family put all necessary precautions into place, including telling my father, "Run for your life."

CHAPTER SEVEN

*Refuge in the village... "Crowing cocks at
dawn and croaking toads at dusk"*

THE EXTENDED FAMILY HAD MET and decided we should
be relocated to one of our ancestral villages. My parents
came from different ones. My maternal grandmother,
who was my only living grandparent, was already in her village
and was hoping we would come and join her. The senior chiefs
in my father's village were looking forward to hosting him, their
illustrious son. Also it would be a good opportunity to discuss the
needs of the village with him firsthand. The head chief was called
the "Enogie." My father was eager to go there and interact with his
people. He had not been back in a long time.

I was hoping we would go to my mother's village so I could
be with my grandmother. I was very fond of her. She named me
Arese, which was an abbreviation of the full name. Names in Benin
were usually abbreviations of phrases or sentences. My full name
was actually a sentence: "Aghariagbonse aikpe ehi." It meant when
someone enters into the world blessed with everything, people
should not envy him or her because it is the destiny of their star.
Benin people attach a lot of significance to one's guardian spirit or
"star," which they refer to as "Ehi." It is believed that "Ehi" not only
determined a person's destiny but also acted as one's guardian here

and beyond. She said even though my mother had hoped she would give birth to another boy but had a fourth girl, that yearning was soon forgotten by the blessing and good fortune that came with my delivery. My father got a promotion, they moved to a bigger house and their wealth increased. My grandmother said my "Ehi" had brought these blessings.

My grandmother knew I loved her stories and truly paid attention to them. She would quiz me on the lessons learned. There were so many folk tales, stories about events, wise sayings and advice, most of which I still remember till this day. One of her favorite slogans that I adopted was "Face Your Own," which we sometimes abbreviated to FYO. It meant you should get on with your life and what you had to do. If you spent your time gossiping and interfering in other people's business then your own would remain unfinished, so you needed to FYO. I have since passed that saying on to my daughter and my eldest niece.

After much deliberation, my parents decided it would be good to go to both villages so my siblings and I could see where some of our ancestors had lived. We first went to my father's ancestral home. An uncle who knew his way came to pick us up and also brought a taxi along. He was not an uncle in the biological sense. I remember every older person was called uncle or aunty. It did not mean they were your parents' sibling. It was a sign of respect that was used in the extended family. It was a taboo for a child to call an adult by name. Even the much older children were referred to as "sister" and "brother," pronounced "sista" and "broda" by the younger children.

My father went in my uncle's car with three of my older siblings. My mother went in the taxi with me and the other three. The journey took about an hour. We first travelled through the city then veered off the main road onto a side one that was very dusty, not tarred, and full of bumps and potholes. In some instances the road seemed like a path in the middle of a thick bush. The trees looked very old and tall. You could not see their tops and their branches provided a lot of shade, though the sun tried to peer through. There were a variety of sounds coming out of the bushes. It seemed like the animal kingdom was having a meeting. We drove slowly, mindful of the goats, chickens and wild guinea fowls. The animals lived in harmony with the villagers, roaming as freely as they pleased.

Finally, we came to a large cleared space in the middle of the bush. The soil all around was red. There were clusters of mud huts and houses with thatched roofs made of straw. One of the first things I noticed was that the huts had no doors. There were doorways and spaces cut out for windows, but they had no doors or windows in them. That struck me as strange. Honesty was such a great policy in those days in the villages. No one stole. Even without doors people's belongings were safe. No one, even mistakenly, took a goat or chicken that was not theirs. The code of honesty combined with the curse and shame of dishonesty took care of that.

The goats seemed to be moving around sluggishly, freely entering the mud huts. Some chickens were perched on the window ledges as if they were enjoying the view. I was still trying to take in everything when the car came to a halt. We had arrived at the hut of the Enogie – the head chief. The wives of the Enogie came out to greet us wearing wrappers tied around their chests and coral beads round their necks. Suddenly a lot of children came running out of the many huts. Some had no clothes on and others just pants. All were barefoot. They seemed happy as they smiled and ran towards the car. Apparently the whole village had been informed that "strangers" were coming to the village and that they should welcome them with great hospitality. As we got out of the cars the Enogie's wives hugged us and spoke our native language to my parents. They greeted us chanting "Ób'ókhían," which means welcome. I did not understand what they were saying. I could not speak Edo properly, though now I speak it fluently.

The children smiled at us and we said hello to them. They giggled and said in Edo "ebo nor wie wie." I asked my mother what that meant and she said it meant "foreign or white people with dark complexion." I asked why they would say that. She said it was a term used when one spoke and behaved in a western way but yet had a dark skin color. Because we did not speak their language, had said hello in a phonetic tone and were dressed differently, they referred to us that way. That was a new phrase to me that I was to hear quite a lot during our stay. The children would soon substitute it for our names and we soon caught on. For short they just said "ebo."

The wives took us into the Enogie's intricately built mud house. The entrance led into a big room with doorways on both sides and straw curtains covering each. These doorways led to the rooms that housed the wives and their children. The Enogie had his own room, which none of the wives was allowed to enter except when he called them or told them to go there. The big central room we entered had a large imposing chair built of mud and draped with a white sheet. This was the Enogie's chair. There was also a mud shelf behind the chair; I was told it was an ancestral altar. On it were clay pots filled with water and several old artifacts including a brass bell. I remember the bell because the Enogie rang it whenever he had finished praying.

One of his wives knocked on a door and informed the head chief we had arrived. He came out with some elderly looking men. He then sat on his high chair and the other men sat on a bench in front of him. The Enogie greeted my uncle who then proceeded to introduce my family. He welcomed us saying that my father was a son of the soil who had returned. The village welcomed us and we should feel at home, safe and secure. The war did not affect the village and they lived in peace, he added.

My father gave the Enogie a bottle of gin, some kola nuts and money, as was the tradition. He thanked my father and began to pray for us, invoking the spirit of our ancestors to partake in the welcoming ceremony. He ended the prayer with 'Long live the King' "Oba ghator okpere." He then rang the altar bell and everyone said "Ise," which is the equivalent of Amen. He broke the kola nut, opened the bottle of gin, poured some on the ground as libation for our ancestors and then poured some into half a coconut shell which acted as a drinking glass. He took a sip and passed it on to the elders. He took a piece of white chalk called *orue* and marked his forehead with it and muttered "*orue* is never used for darkness but for celebration." Traditional prayers were said for the health and safety of everyone present. The ceremony was over, homage had been paid to the elders and our ancestors. It was important that their tradition of welcoming strangers to their village was adhered to. Whenever the Enogie was having a ceremony, many villagers flocked to the front of his hut to catch a glimpse of what was transpiring.

We later left the head chief's hut with my uncle and walked a few meters down to his. Even though my uncle shuttled between town and the village, his hut looked pretty much the same as the others. There were no signs of urban architecture or modernization. It was as if the village had a building code that required conformity in housing. In those days, it was important to blend into the village and not stand out. They preferred the status quo.

When we got to my uncle's hut, my siblings and I were in shock. I could not believe this was where we were going to be living. That was my first exposure to going without basic necessities. We were going to be living like the rest of the villagers! My uncle showed us round. Adults or taller children needed to bend their heads when going through the low doorways. The layout of the hut was similar to the Enogie's, with an entrance leading to the large common room off of which were bedrooms. My uncle had two wives whose rooms were on one side of the hut. Polygamy was very common in the village. It was believed that a man had to have many wives so he would have a lot of people and children to serve him. Also, the men felt it helped to keep the women in check if they had competition from other wives. My uncle had two rooms of his own, one of which had been cleared for my parents to use. The raised mud bed was built into one side of the wall. We children slept on mats in the central common room.

There was neither running water nor electricity in the village. Rainwater was collected in drums and containers that were topped off with water gathered from the river by women and little children. When it got dark, kerosene lanterns were lit. My mother had packed several torchlights and given her children one each. We were to make sure we always had them with us at night. What shocked me the most was the sanitation system. There were no toilets! My uncle's wife took us to the back of the house. Way back by the bushes were two pit latrines. One was for females and one was for males. I was told men and women were not allowed to share the same pit latrines due to traditional beliefs. It was a taboo for a man to come in contact with a woman during certain periods of her menstrual cycle.

It was the first time I had seen pit latrines, which were just deep holes dug in the ground. One thing I learned was that, in time of war, survival trumps basic necessities or luxuries. My older sister who was attending boarding school in England during the school year was terrified she would fall into one. She lost a lot of weight because of her refusal to eat much so she would not have to use the toilet pit while we were in the village.

The first night was the strangest and most difficult. Once it was dusk the toads began to croak in unison. It was as if they were talking to each other. I listened to them till late into the very hot and clammy night. As I lay on the mat I could feel the mosquito bites and literally had to cover my whole body and face with a cloth before I could catch a wink of sleep. Thank God my parents made sure we were on prophylaxis antimalarial drugs and worm expellers[16].

16 Daraprim was the antimalarial prophylaxis and was taken once a week on

In a couple of days, I had gotten used to the toads croaking and the mosquitoes biting. I was told the hissing noise I sometimes heard was that of a large snake they had not been able to catch and that it had once come into one of the huts but was very elusive. Luckily I never saw it. I did however once see a tiny long green snake. The children I was playing with shouted "*Eyen, Eyen*" which means "snake, snake." An older child got a stick, picked up the reptile, which she said was a harmless green snake, and threw it back into the bushes. These village children could handle nature and the animals with such ease. They could run after chickens and catch them, the chickens flapping their wings finally becoming still as if in submission.

At the crack of dawn the cocks would start crowing. They were as reliable as an alarm clock. Everyone would get up, rinse their face, clean their feet and after exchanging salutations, begin the daily chores. Each family had a salutation. This identified the family one descended from. In the morning people would greet each other with their family salutation. Younger ones would kneel and greet their elders with their salutation. The family salutation for my father's family was 'Lagiewan' and that of my mother's family was 'Labvieze'. My father's family salutation was used in our home.

The local kids taught us how to clean our teeth with chewing sticks. They simply broke twigs off a tree, scraped the bark off and chewed on the tip till it was soft enough to rub the teeth and gum clean. My chore was to help sweep inside and outside the mud house. To prevent the dust from coming up, water was first sprinkled on the floor and then it was swept with a traditional broom.

The women prepared breakfast at the back of the house on an open wood fire. The cooking area was a mud room with mud fire places that had an opening where the wood was placed. They were built in such a way that they could hold large black earthenware

Sundays. Combantrin was the worm expeller and a one-time dose was taken every six months.

pots on top of the fire. The children and women were skilled at starting the fire. They would pile little dry twigs together, add coconut shaft, strike a match on the pile and blow on it gently till the all the embers were alight. Then they would begin to pile more twigs and finally the logs of wood. The air would be full of smoke, which usually made my eyes irritable and sometimes teary.

All the children ate from a communal pot. There were neither dining tables laid out, nor an individual seat and plate for each child. The communal pot was placed on the floor; we all gathered around it and you had to eat as quickly as you could if you wanted to get any food at all. No one was allowed to touch the meat or whatever protein there was on the plate till the end of the meal. My uncle's senior wife saw we were not adept at the communal eating way of life and feared we would hardly get any food to eat so she decided she would set a pot aside for us to eat from. My mother asked my uncle's wives not to give us any preferential treatment. She did not want to disrupt their routine and she wanted us to adapt and live like the rest. Only adults had their food dished out for them. The men were given the best and first choice and were served like kings.

After breakfast, the children would go down to the river to bathe and fetch water to fill the drums. My mother feared the river currents and waterborne diseases and therefore did not allow us to have our bath in the stream. Instead, we had to use buckets of water that had been strained and heated. This was among the things that for health and safety reasons my parents did not compromise while we were in the village. After having their baths the children would fill all the buckets and carry them back. The village children would balance the buckets on their heads easily; I would hold on to the handle of a bucket to carry it. Half the water usually spilled before I got back. I did learn, however, after several tries, how to balance a bucket of water on my head.

My father taught the villagers about sedimentation, filtration and boiling in order to purify the water. He said they should leave the water they collect for some time for the particles to settle at the bottom, then filter their water with a white cloth after which the water should be boiled till it is boiling hot and bubbling. The water should then be allowed to cool before drinking or cooking with it.

My mother, having studied nursing and midwifery in England, abhorred the practice of female genital mutilation (FGM). She educated families in the village against it due to the health dangers involved. Later, as a physician and public health consultant, I researched and wrote a paper on ways to abolish the last vestige of the practice by education while also taking into account the cultural significance women and families attach to it, thus necessarily finding an alternative non-mutilating method to represent a woman's rite of passage.

Life was communal. It was as if the villagers were one big family. The school nearest to the village had been closed because of the war. Since education was not compulsory, not all the children went to school. They helped out around the house and on the farm. The men would go to the farm with some of the older children for the whole day during sowing or harvesting season and return home in the evening with foodstuffs such as cassava and yam tubers at harvest. The women would process the cassava into *garri* (dried, flaked cassava or tapioca), which they took to the city to sell.

The children loved to play outside. If a child was outside and was upset you would hear the youngster crying, screaming and shouting out "Iye," the Edo word for mother. In an instant you would see several of the mothers run outside towards the child, asking what was wrong. One would wipe away the tears and allow the child to blow snot into her wrapper. Another would calm him or her down as he or she reported what the problem was. Unless you knew who the child's biological mother was, you would not be able to tell. When the birth mother returned, the other mothers would relate what happened to her and how it was sorted out. She usually would be satisfied. The whole village felt vested in the raising of all the children. With each child's success, the village felt successful and proud. With each child's failure, the village felt they had failed and felt ashamed.

There was no such thing as minding one's own business in the village. There was nothing private, news spread very quickly. Everything was shared, the highs and lows. Individual joy and pain was also shared communally. It was as if the village believed that no one should feel alone and each individual's life journey should be part of the community's journey. The villagers believed in consensus. When there were disputes amongst the wives or a domestic issue, they were quickly solved by the head of the household. The Enogie and council of elders settled all other disputes.

In the evening a large fire would be lit in front of the cluster of village huts. Women would gather round roasting fish or bush meat on a stick. I wondered why it was called bush meat and I was told it was the meat of any animal big or small that ran freely in the bush. Usually traps were set to catch them. Men would sit in groups discussing issues of the village while drinking palm wine or local gin (*Ogogoro*). Due to its potency and sometimes the altercations that occur from being intoxicated, Ogogoro is also nicknamed "push me I push you." Children would play nearby, being careful not to go too close to the fire. Sometimes the children would be gathered together and one of the elders would tell folk tales. My mother would translate what they were saying, although increasingly I did not need her to translate. I was beginning to understand Edo. The children were teaching us Edo and we were teaching them English. They could speak *brokin* English (*Pidgin),* but were eager to speak it the way we did.

I loved listening to folk tales and the wisdom they imparted, and also the numerous wise saying of the elders. My favorite was the legend of how the guinea fowl got its spots; I was intrigued the first time I heard it. The tale is as follows:

The Benin Kingdom's first dynasty was that of the Ogiso, who were kings of the sky. They created all things on earth and also the gods of the elements and metals: Eziza (god of tornados), Olokun (goddess of the sea), Ogun (god of iron), Isango (god of thunder and lightning). When a disagreement broke out among the gods, the animals were questioned about it by the Ogiso.

Only the guinea fowl told the truth. The other animals hated and envied the bird for being truthful and cursed it, saying it would have spots and run around with no direction.

The guinea fowl was accursed until one day it mistakenly ran into a trap set by the tornado god, Eziza. The gods had heard a rumour that the animals had refused to honor Ogiso, who was the supreme god (King of the sky) and had created them. As the fiercest god, Eziza had been given the task of rounding up all the animals and getting to the bottom of the matter. Eziza set traps and eventually caught the guinea fowl, hen, pigeon and other animals. When questioned, the hen, to secure its freedom and also out of hatred, told a lie against the guinea fowl, blaming it for dishonoring Ogiso. The pigeon and guinea fowl told the truth. The hen was cursed by the gods for lying.

To reward the guinea fowl for its truthfulness, Eziza lifted the curse placed on it by the other animals. Its spots would no longer be a blemish but things of beauty. It would henceforth be more prized than the hen. Eziza also blessed the pigeon for telling the truth, saying that it would no longer carry the loads of others. Both its hands will always be filled with gifts to take home, and the pigeon will always have a place of honour.

The Benin people have used that parable to form a prayer: "Whatever people want to use to diminish or destroy me, may it become a beauty and success for me." The modern day equivalent would be receiving bitter lemons but being able to turn them into lemonade.

After a while, my father decided we should go to my grandmother's village. He felt having her around would be comforting to us. When we left, my mother gave some of her traditional wrappers to the wives of the uncle whose hut we stayed in, and to some of my other aunts. And so we departed my father's village.

My feelings were mixed as we filed into the car to leave. I kept looking at the faces of the new friends I had made. I would miss hearing them shout "ebo" when calling me. I would miss the giggling as they tried to imitate our phonetic tone. I watched the children as they pushed their bodies against the car half hoping we would not leave. As the car was about to start they moved away and watched it slowly drive down the dusty road. I looked back and saw them running behind the car, smiling, waving and shouting "ebo, oyian zekpe" which meant "ebo, till we meet again."

The car turned around a corner that led out of the village. I could no longer see them. I turned my head back and looked ahead. I already was missing them. There was some beauty in the simplicity of their lives, living in harmony with nature. I wondered if I would ever see them again. It would not be until thirty years later, in 1997, at my father's funeral in Benin City, when they came to perform the traditional rites. Some of them now had children of their own whom they introduced to me. Ironically, their offspring had no interest in the serenity of village life and most of their conversations were on how they would love to come to America. The new generation was no longer satisfied to live forgotten in some village. They wanted to experience the outside world.

CHAPTER EIGHT

Village to village... The bluebird of Happiness

MY GRANDMOTHER HAD TWO VILLAGES. The first one was called "Iguwe ayanwen" which translates into the village of birds. It was so named because when the first settlers came to that site, the sky was filled with birds that instructed the elders to settle there. My grandmother knew a lot about birds. She said the sighting of birds had different connotations. When sighted, the bird of prophesy was widely believed by the Benin people to predict doom. Her favorite bird was the bluebird; its sighting she told me connotes happiness and good things. I began to watch for the bluebird. During the war, thought of the bluebird was a happy place I could go to in my imagination. Several years later, as a doctor, the first car I bought was a Datsun Blue Bird. Subconsciously, because of what my grandmother had told me, I must have associated the word bluebird with happiness and good fortune.

We arrived at "Iguwe ayanwen" in the afternoon, but we were told my grandmother had left that village and had gone to one nearer the city called "Iyekogba," which translates into behind Ogba. This village was so named because its location was behind the Ogba River where people commonly worshiped Olokun, the goddess of the water. We were told that before we left the village for

Iyekogba we must pay homage to the Enogie of Iguwe ayanwen. We were taken to him for blessings. The format and the prayers seemed similar to what took place at my father's village. As a matter of fact the two villages seemed very comparable. The mud huts looked the same, the way the people dressed, women tying wrappers round their chest and men covering their bodies with a cloth tied around their necks. The children were mostly naked and barefoot, with little pants or shorts.

As soon as we left the Enogie's hut we went to greet some uncles and aunts who then gave us a guide to take us to my grandmother. At my grandmother's second village the welcome ceremonies were pretty much the same, but we were not shocked this time. It was obvious the village was beginning to embrace some habits of the city it was so close to. Some of the mud huts were actually plastered and had wooden doors and windows that opened and shut.

My mother's sister knew our favorite native meals and, as soon as we arrived, began to prepare them for us. The sleeping arrangement for the children was the same but this time at night thin pieces of foam were scattered on the floor for us to sleep on. They even lit mosquito coils to drive away the bugs. My mother's sister tried to make us as comfortable as possible.

There were also tales by the moonlight. One of the stories I remember was the mythological folk tale about the gods of the elements. I listened as someone told the legend of Eziza in our native language. As I listened eagerly I could pick up part of the story and asked my mother to fill in what I did not understand. My mother had heard the story as a child and knew it. Eziza was the name given to the Tornado god. Of all the elements, Eziza was the most powerful and destructive. When in motion, it moved about freely in spirit form as a very strong wind that could not be stopped. It had no known home. It destroyed anything in its path, swirling and carrying it away. Compared to Eziza a lot of the other elements were like child's play; no other element could match up to it. Isango (god of thunder and lightning) admired Eziza and usually followed closely behind it, mindful not to get in Eziza's way.

Oto (the ground) and Okun (the sky) were curious about Eziza and decided they were going to find Eziza and battle it into submission. The gods of other elements and elders advised them not to because the power of Eziza could not be stopped. They were told that nothing had ever battled Eziza successfully. They were mere children compared to Eziza, and children should not initiate a battle. Oto and Okun ignored these warnings. Unfortunately for them when they did find Eziza, it was so powerful that it took them both and swirled them with other things in its path into a funnel as it moved along destroying everything in its path. When Oto and Okun did not return the other elements and elders realized what had happened. From that day Oto and Okun could not escape Eziza. Whenever Eziza moved it carried them along. Eziza would forever start in the sky all the way down to the ground. It became even more powerful now that it had the clouds and the ground swept into its funnel. It was determined that nothing could stop its power nor the destruction it left in its path. Nothing else has ever tried to challenge Eziza for fear they too may get sucked into its funnel.

The story teller ended by singing an Edo chorus that the elders had used to warn Oto and Okun not to go to battle with Eziza. My mother and some of the older children joined the chorus as I listened:

> "**Aweyo, Aweyo**
> **Eziza ologhogbe**
> **Ovbokhan isiokhuo Eziza**
> **Eziza ologhogbe**
> **Ovbokhan yiokhuo Eziza**
> **Eziza ologhogbe**
> **Eyo, eyo**
> **Eziza ologhogbe........"**

(The translation of original lyrics for the Edo chorus)
"We are saying don't go, don't go,
Eziza is too difficult,
Children do not initiate battle with Eziza,
Eziza is too difficult,
Children do not go to battle with Eziza.
Eziza is too difficult,
So don't go, don't go
Eziza is too difficult."

My grandmother was eager to get back to the city as she was no longer used to village life. She had left the village at a young age. In those days, maidens had to be virgins or were regarded as being promiscuous. They found it difficult to marry due to rejection by families of potential spouses. She had later married my grandfather, who was a business tycoon with status, lots of properties and money. She believed had she not been a virgin she would never have been allowed to marry him.

Grandmother was drawn to city life. There she would wake up early, have her bath and put on her fine traditional robes. She wrapped a head-tie made of a material called *Igbeigbe* around her head. Her face was always made up, with natural cosmetics from herbs and trees. She would have a smoky eye shadow around her eyes, a brownish foundation on her face (nicknamed pancake) and some orange powdery stuff on her cheeks that was her rouge. My grandmother believed it was always important to be clean, fresh, well-groomed and well-dressed. She believed that even during difficult and trying times one should never be seen unkempt. She felt that appearing disheveled signaled inner and outer troubles. On the other hand, being well-groomed gave an air of everything being fine, an important impression to project to the outside world.

At home in the city, my grandmother loved to sit outside on the porch that extended almost on to the street. If building regulations existed then, they were probably not enforced. As she sat on the porch she would watch the cars as they drove by or the people as they walked by. Everyone who plied that street knew her and as they passed they would kneel, curtsy or bow their heads in respect as they greeted her: "*Kóyò íyé,*" meaning 'Hello, mother.' She would reply "*Kóyò oviewen,*" meaning 'Hello, my child.' Respect was very important in those days. It was rude to walk by the elderly without greeting them. People believed the curse or prayers of the elders were very powerful.

I loved sitting with my grandmother on the porch and playing the board game Ludo. I knew the golden rule - she must always win. My grandmother missed her old city routine and, even though it could not be exactly the same because Benin was occupied by Biafran forces, she wanted to go back.

My family and I spent a few more days in her village. Although it was more comfortable than at my uncle's, it still had its discomforts and we longed to return home. We still had to use pit latrines and there was no running water. If you wanted to take a bath every day you had to fetch your water from the river. On the upside, however, it was never lonely, everything was communal. Folktales were told by moonlight as people sat around an open fire, looking up into the sky and counting the stars. The air outside was fresh and the breeze cool. Children played with sticks drawing pictures on the ground. We picked ripe fruit right off the trees. Cooked food was fresh and wholesome from the farm and prepared in earthenware pots on an open fire. This gave it a nice smoky flavor.

Departing each village, we left behind some of our clothes and basics such as bathing soap, biscuits and sweets to be shared amongst the children we played with. They all came out to say goodbye and stand around the car. My father would give each child a coin. They would be so happy because a coin could buy a lot in those days but, most of all, they had learned to be grateful for little.

Being in the village had its highs and lows. I learned so much and appreciated the wisdom and experience I had gained. Most of all I was thankful that as a family we were together and that my parents were there to guide us through the change.

CHAPTER NINE

Back to the city... The plot is revealed

MY UNCLE STILL WENT INTO the city frequently and returned in the evenings. He usually brought back information he had gathered there. The evening before we left my grandmother's village, my uncle came searching for us. He looked worried. He told my parents that he had heard the rumour that very soon the Biafran soldiers were going to start searching all villages to root out people they perceived as either traitors to their cause, or federal civil servants whom they wanted to convert to Biafran government service. He said the Biafran soldiers also heard rumours that some people were passing information to Federal troops, who were preparing for a counter invasion of Benin. The Biafrans were determined to root out all traitors or suspects.

In the village it would be very easy to pick out someone who did not belong or fit in and it would be obvious the person was trying to hide. My uncle felt it was no longer a safe or wise option for my family to remain. My parents told him that the family was already planning to return to the city the next day, where we would lie low till a plan was figured out. My father's decision that we would return to the city was perfectly timed. From what my uncle said, it was clear the village could no longer save us.

Early the next morning, just as the village women were

carrying their goods to market, we, along with my grandmother, rode back to Benin City. The trip was quiet and tense. There seemed to be so many more soldiers in the city. As we passed the checkpoints mounted on the major roads, I remember my parents being questioned by some of the fierce-looking soldiers. We said we were coming from the village where we were visiting some of our aged relatives. At one checkpoint, my father seemed to have been questioned in depth. The soldier then asked him to report to some army barrack before the end of the week as registration of all civilian adult men was mandatory.

When we finally arrived home, my father seemed extremely agitated. My mother also could not camouflage her anxiety. I remember my mother urging him not to report to the army barrack. She feared he would be conscripted into the Biafran army or would simply never be seen again. She'd heard that some top Benin civil servants had already disappeared and their families were not sure what had happened to them. My mother realized my siblings and I had overheard her so she quickly told us not to worry and that everything would be fine. I asked her if our father was going to become a soldier. She said "No." One of my sisters began to cry, she said, "I don't want daddy to become a soldier and carry a gun."

The house seemed different. The grass was overgrown. The windows were all covered with the red dusty Benin soil. The place looked abandoned. My father decided it should be kept looking that way. As soon as we were inside, my mother sent us to take a shower and brush our teeth. I really appreciated being able to take a nice warm shower and to have clean water flowing out of the taps. I never took running water for granted again after experiencing what villagers have to go through to get water that is not even clean. I began to understand why my father as a water engineer told us from a young age to conserve water to avoid a water shortage. That night after dinner we went to bed very early. My grandmother spent the next few nights with us, sleeping in our room. I really found it comforting to have her around.

Much seemed to have happened while we were away in the villages. The atmosphere in the city was increasingly tense. The soldiers seemed fiercer. A dusk to dawn curfew had been imposed and was strictly enforced. Violators were reported to have been shot. The Biafrans had become paranoid. They believed they had credible information that Federal troops were about to stage a counter invasion. They felt the Federal troops must have accomplices and were determined to root them out.

The Biafran soldiers began to search every nook and corner, going from door to door. They would arrive in lorry loads on a street, close it down and restrict movement. Then they would disperse to different houses banging on the doors and asking for the man of the house and how many people lived there. Thankfully, they did not get to our home till about a week later.

Some groups of native Benin people established a network of informants. Their activities had to be a covert affair. They gathered information and found a way to inform Benin families by word of mouth what the Biafrans were planning. The informants varied in age, sex and occupation. They included older children, young male and female adults, elder ones and market women. My family informant was a young male cousin and an aunty who sold goods in the market. It was too dangerous for just any adult to deliver the information without arousing suspicion. Messages would be given to older children who hawked goods on their heads during the day.

A few days after my family had arrived back in the city, we were awakened one morning by my informant cousin and aunt who had both independently heard a rumour and decided it was imperative to warn my father. The complete list of those to be killed had been finalized. It contained the names of men who were top federal or state civil servants. The emphasis was on those who had not reported to the army barracks to register and those that were suspected of passing information to the Federal troops. The Biafrans were to identify the location of everyone on the list and pick them up at their various houses or offices. The detainees would then be taken to secret locations to be executed.

My father said this rumour had been going on for quite a long time and that was why we had gone to the villages, but now even the villages were no longer safe. He said another plan would have to be devised to assure our safety. My cousin said he had seen my father's name on the list along with that of one of my uncles, who was a judge. My aunty had not seen the list but said that the same rumour was floating around the market. She suggested that to avoid the whole family being in danger the best option was for my father to leave Benin. As was the custom, she would discuss it with the extended family members so a decision could be made and an escape planned.

CHAPTER TEN

The escape is planned... Who goes and who stays?

M Y PARENTS CAREFULLY ANALYZED AND thought through the decision on who would embark on the escape journey. It was by no means the luck of the draw nor was it names pulled out of a hat. The escape would be by boat, and only four spaces could be secured on it for our family. The vessels were basic fishermen's boats, little more than large canoes with no amenities. As people were desperately trying to escape the war zone there was a high demand for spaces and the fee was very high.

From what I saw as a child, the war brought out different reactions and decisions in the populace. There were those who had nowhere to escape to and, even if they did, they could not afford the passage. There were those who felt they had lived in Benin all their lives. They were born there and would die there. Escaping to or dying in a foreign place was not an option. Then there were those who, like my parents, were more cosmopolitan, and had studied, lived or worked for many years outside Benin. Although they had an emotional attachment to their homeland, they were ready to escape the war zone if they could financially afford to do so. Amongst foreigners, ninety-nine percent were ready to be evacuated. The few who decided to remain included nuns, priests,

International Red Cross workers and those who felt it was their moral obligation to stay in their "adopted" homeland.

My family decided that since our lives were in danger, we should escape as soon as possible, but not all at the same time and on different boats. It was clear that fleeing the rebels was as dangerous as staying behind, if not worse. My father decided to split the family up. One half would stay and the other would embark on the treacherous escape journey. My parents now had to make wrenchingly painful decisions. Who would go and who would stay? There were great risks but they hoped that, at worst, one half of the family would survive to carry on the family name.

My father believed passionately in the importance of passing down the family legacy from generation to generation. If he did not survive, he was confident that my mother would ensure that his principles and beliefs would be instilled in those who did. The responsibility of carrying on the family name lay on the shoulders of the male children. The male child is very important in the African tradition. Some women have been thrown out by their husbands for not bearing one. My parents had two sons and five daughters. My father believed in female empowerment and assured that my sisters and I got the same educational opportunities as my brothers. For him, education was the gateway to freedom and opportunity. However, when it came to carrying on the family name he realized that in our society that could only be done through his sons. Thus one of my brothers would escape and one would remain. My family surname when translated meant "honesty." There is a lot to be said in a given name and sometimes it tends to shape who we become. My father prided himself in being honest and lived up to the meaning of his name. He always told us integrity was better than riches.

My father had to leave because he was a senior federal civil servant and was allegedly on the executioner's list. My mother could not swim and hated even going near water. My father, on the other hand, was an excellent swimmer, a talent he had honed as a child growing up in a village near a river. His elementary school was on the other side of the waterway. By swimming there instead, he saved the money he was given to pay for the ferry to his school. He believed that if the escape boat should capsize, he and the children with him could at least swim or stay afloat.

My parents chose my older brother to accompany my father. My parents felt he would best be able to withstand the rigours of this strenuous journey. Schooling was another factor. My older brother was in boarding school in England. He needed to get back as soon as the summer vacation was over so he would not have to repeat a class. He was also a good swimmer and took regular lessons. This was important, as a good portion of the trip would be on water. My younger brother attended Corona school with me and was in the junior school. He could easily be taught at home during the war, so he would stay behind with my mother.

In addition to my older brother, my two older sisters, who were good swimmers, were also going to accompany my father. One, who was the eldest of my siblings, was preparing for her fifth form WASC (West African School Certificate) external exams. It was imperative that she take them in order to go on to the sixth form and thence, after two years, to university. The other sister was in boarding school in England. She had found the whole series of events traumatic, especially when we were in the village. She was very attached to my father. Even as a young child she always preferred being carried by him and was fond of saying "daddy, carry me" whenever any strangers or visitors were around.

My mother was to hold the fort in Benin. She was not a civil servant and had become a full-time housewife so it was felt that she was not in any direct or imminent risk. She had been both a qualified teacher and a nurse before she became a full time housewife. Her two professions would prove to be very useful. She would home school those of us staying behind and could also take care of our health problems. She knew how to be diplomatic and enchanting in any situation. Hating the water as she did, there was no way she would consider making so treacherous a trip in a small boat, even if it meant escaping from hostile invaders. Another older sister of mine was to stay behind as well.

I was also chosen to stay. Because I was one of the younger ones, my parents felt I could miss school for some time and be successfully home-schooled. My father said he would inform the headmistress of my school of the decision, if and when they got to Lagos. I was very fidgety, active and inquisitive. I found it difficult to sit in one place for a long time and I was worried about the trip my father and some of my sisters and brother were about to embark on. I, also, was not a good swimmer. My father had been trying in vain to teach me. When he was chief engineer of Iju waterworks in Lagos, he used to take us out at weekends to the private pool there to teach us swimming. I was so afraid of water that I would hold on to my father and scream, "Daddy, don't leave me, hold me tight." My mother would be watching from the poolside, sitting on a deck chair. Even though she felt it was important that I learn how to swim, she would ask my father to bring me out of the water whenever I appeared too petrified. In times of crisis I seemed always to look to her for assurance and she seemed to be the only one who could calm my fears. The Biafran occupation was a frightening moment in time, and I needed to be around my mother. I was glad to be staying.

The twins, a boy and a girl, were my younger siblings. They definitely were to stay behind. The journey was too treacherous. It would be nearly impossible to get to the riverbank in the middle of the night and avoid the Rebel soldiers with two little children in tow.

Once the decisions were made, things moved very quickly. The cash for the passage had been given to a middleman, who would act as a guide. The family was called together and my parents unveiled the escape plan: who would go, who would stay and the reasons why.

The dangerous trip would begin the next night. This night would be the last we would all be together till, or if ever, we were reunited. That realization was underscored by a huge thunderstorm. We could hear the rolling thunder and the lightning hit the bungalow's aluminum roofing sheets. The rain poured down from the sky as if the gods were also at war. The god of thunder and lightning is a fierce warrior called Sango by the Yoruba, and Isango by the Benin. It was as if he were making a dramatic statement. I was relieved it was not happening the next day when half of my family would be beginning their escape journey. I was thankful to be staying behind with my mother. Whenever she reassured me that everything would be all right, I knew it would be so. Also I had no desire to trek through snake-infested bushes at night and spend days on a small boat, even if it meant escaping from a war-torn zone.

CHAPTER ELEVEN

The Separation...the message and the passage

I T WAS SO LATE AT night even the toads had stopped croaking and gone to sleep. My parents came into the room where my brothers, sisters and I had gathered. We were filled with anxiety and uncertainty. My eldest sister reassured us that everything would be a "piece of cake" and we would all soon be together. My older brother who looked and spoke like a typical British prep school boy seemed a bit dazed, but he had been told to liken the escape journey to one of his school camping expeditions that he would be able to write about later. My older sister seemed eager about the trip. She wanted to go with my father. She was used to being in boarding school in England and had found the time we spent in the village a horrible experience. She felt the whole war was insane and she wanted to get not just out of Benin, but Nigeria itself. Since childhood, she had really not felt comfortable in Nigeria and later in life she settled overseas, having never gotten over the trauma of the war.

When my parents walked into the room, my father looked lovingly at all of us and said "the time has come." We all knew what that meant. It was like the parting of ways. Those of us staying behind stood on one side with my mother, and those embarking on the journey stood beside my father.

My mother kept holding back her tears, and she put on a brave face as she tried to reassure her departing children that all would be fine. She hugged and kissed each of them and prayed for them both in English and our native language, Edo. The English prayer we all understood, but the one offered up in Edo was deeply emotional. It was as if she was crying out to the spirits of our ancestors to be their guide and guard, while leading them to safety. As was customary, she ended with "Long Live the King." I wondered why whenever prayers and supplications were made to the ancestral spirits they were always spoken in the native dialect. I remember once asking if the ancestral spirits did not understand English.

My father embraced each of us staying behind. He admonished the younger ones to be good and to listen to me. He told the twins not to quarrel. They should make sure they did their lessons daily and should always remember that he was thinking of them. After discussing a few mundane things, he took a deep breath and turned to me. He hugged me then looked me straight in the face and called my name as if to reinforce my presence and what he was about to say. He told me he would miss me a lot and joked that he would have no one to tell him the gossip until we met again in Lagos. He asked me to be a good girl and stay out of trouble. He was depending on me and I had to make sure I helped my mother. I looked into my father's eyes, taking in every word, and trying to search his soul to see if I could read what was really going on. I was jolted back as I heard him say, "Look after your younger siblings. They are defenseless. You must defend the defenseless."

I looked at my younger siblings and suddenly I felt this huge sense of responsibility at my young age of nine. My father had charged me with a duty; I could not and would not let him down. My preoccupation would be protecting and defending them, watching over them and reassuring them. I had no time to worry about myself. I could not let them ever see me afraid. I was determined to carry out the duty my father bequeathed to me.

My father finally went to my mother, hugged and kissed her, then gave her a faint smile. He referred to her in a traditional way by saying in Edo "the mother of my children" It was as if he were laying emphasis on children and the strong bond parents have. He told her how much she meant to him and lovingly recited her wonderful qualities. I guess he wanted her to know how much he appreciated her in case that was their last encounter.

My father urged my mother to "be brave and tune in to the radio daily to keep abreast of current events." From that day my mother listened to the radio daily. As a matter of fact she had the radio on in the background constantly. We all hugged quickly once more. My mother asked those of us staying behind to remain in the room. Deep down I felt this crushing pain knowing I may never see them again.

I heard the back door open. As I peeped through the bedroom window into the hallway, I saw a man who looked like a truck driver because of the keys he had hanging from his neck. He was speaking to my parents, explaining the procedure. Apparently, he was the guide and would hide them in his vehicle and take them to the edge of the bush where he would hand them over to another guide who would lead them by foot to the edge of the river bank. There my father and siblings would be united with other escapees from other locations. All of them would be handed over to the fisherman who owned the boat that would carry them down the river.

Without much ado, after the explanation my father took my elder brother's hand on one side and my older sister's on the other and marched out into the night without looking back, my eldest sister walking by their side. Their perilous journey had begun.

CHAPTER TWELVE

Life in a war-torn zone...Learning to survive

I WOKE UP EARLY THE NEXT morning feeling empty and strange. It suddenly dawned on me that my father and one of my brothers and two of my sisters were not around. I thought I had dreamt it, but it was all too real. They had left for an unknown journey in the middle of the night. I wondered if I would ever see them again. I was so afraid and yet I knew I had to be brave and had to defend my younger siblings. I could not forget my father's request that I defend the defenseless. I watched the twins still sleeping. They looked so peaceful.

My mother was in her room. I went to her and curled into her bed. It's so vivid in my mind. I still remember my head on her chest, my ears listening to her heartbeat as if making sure she was really there and it was not an illusion. I told her I was afraid but I did not want to be. In her usual manner she told me everything would be fine and there was no need to worry. As she stroked my head, I thought to myself, nothing is more comforting than the reassuring tender touch of a loving mother. I suddenly felt relieved and smiled at her as I wiped tears away from my eyes. She sent me back to my room so I would be there when my little brother and sister woke up. My mother always seemed so brave and calm. I felt so blessed to have her. As I reflect back, I marvel at how well she masked her own anxieties while putting on a reassuring face for us.

We stayed indoors all day as the hours dragged by very slowly. Diligently remembering what my father had said, my mother had the main radio on in the background. There was a table in the long hallway that we used for dining. My mother had put a smaller radio on the table and left it on all day. Today that radio would look like an antique. The casing was brown. It had a rectangular handle and was very heavy. There were ivory-looking knobs in front for tuning into stations. It had a very long silver antenna and a beige fabric-like cover on the speaker. A detailed news report was broadcast at 6am, 8am and 6pm. My mother always listened carefully as if she were expecting to hear something specific.

Later at night, I heard a knock on the back door. There were seven taps, which made it sound like a pre-arranged code. My mother went to the door and asked in Edo "Ani hin?" - "Who is that?" Our security guard who we called "Baba night watchman" answered that he was there with the guide who had left with my father the previous day. I should have been asleep, but instead I was peeping through a window overlooking the hallway. My mother anxiously began to unbolt the large bolts and unlock the padlock. At night every exterior door was locked with massive bolts on top, in the middle, and the bottom, and then a padlock. The key was left inside, right beside the door on the floor, so the nannies could open them early in the morning if they needed to. Securing ourselves inside was necessary to prevent intruders from entering. With all those locks if there had ever been a fire at night it would have been difficult getting out. Thankfully, there was none.

The guide came into the hallway and told my mother that he had escorted my father and the children all the way to the riverside and handed them over to the fisherman whose boat was going to take them through the creeks to Lagos. The journey had been very dangerous and they could hear shooting in the background. It seemed that the Biafrans were aware that people were trying to escape through the creeks so there was a much larger presence of soldiers around the area. He didn't know whether they were just shooting to scare people or if they were aiming to wound or kill potential escapees. Since he was well acquainted with the locale he was able to take his group through a different path so that they were not spotted.

My mother asked about my siblings, how they had held out during the journey. He said it was a very difficult journey for them but that they were fine. They had been particularly bothered by the sounds of the owls and the hissing of the snakes but my father had reassured them. My mother wanted to know when he would hear from the fisherman to see how the river trip had gone. She was fretful about their safety and needed that reassurance, if possible, that they had safely arrived. The guide said he did not know because once the fishermen got to Lagos most of them did not return. My mother realized we would have to wait indefinitely to get any news. She thanked him profusely for coming to give a report back, prayed for him and gave him some money. The guide said he was leading another group through the forest the next night and so had to visit a few houses that night. He thanked my mother and told her not to be too worried. He turned round and disappeared into the darkness of the night.

I was surprised I could understand a good deal of what he was saying. It seemed I had picked up so much of our native language from our stay in the village and constantly hearing people speak it. As my mother turned around she noticed me staring through my bedroom window. She came in, kissed me and tucked me in under the mosquito net. She said it was late and reassured me everything would be fine and that I should get some sleep. I lay in bed, my mind restless, ticking like a clock non-stop till I dozed off. Even though I am usually a light sleeper, I must have been so emotionally exhausted that I fell into a deep slumber. Usually the slightest movement or noise would wake me up but that morning it was only the aroma of my favorite breakfast that could do so.

The younger children were already up and playing around. I rushed, brushed my teeth and had a bath so I could sit down to breakfast. My mother said we would start having lessons for three hours every day and she would give us homework for the next day. She soon got us into a routine. An hour after breakfast on weekdays we would be taught for two hours, then break for about an hour before we would have another hour of schooling.

My mother tried to ensure normalcy as best as she could under the circumstances. After lunch we took a compulsory siesta. She would make us lie in bed whether we were feeling sleepy or not. The evening was left for playing and homework. At night we would have prayer time before going to bed. Days and weeks went by with the same routine, my mother bravely holding down the fort. I became preoccupied with protecting my younger siblings, defending them, reassuring them and sometimes watching over them during the day and sometimes at night as they slept. I remember whenever we played in the garden, if we heard the sound of gunfire, I would shout "Shelling, take cover," and then make sure we all got back into the house quickly.

The situation in Benin was worsening. Cash was in short supply. Biafran soldiers allegedly had raided the Central Bank and taken the available cash. Some people began to barter for goods. Terrible stories began filtering in: people being rounded up and killed; young girls being raped; properties being seized to be used to quarter the Biafran soldiers. There were even rumours that some girls were offering themselves as "sacrificial lambs" to the soldiers so their families could be protected.

My mother told us that if soldiers ever came to the house, we should not answer any questions but leave her to do the talking. She told us all, including the nannies and drivers, never to say that my father had been in Benin and escaped. She said we should say we were the only ones in the house and we lived in Benin while my father lived in Lagos and that we were not in contact with him. She said in a way that was accurate. She told us it was important we keep quiet about the truth regarding my father's getaway. During a war, sometimes survival and protecting loved ones depended on being strategically silent about certain facts.

CHAPTER THIRTEEN

Love and Hate…crossing and building boundaries

"NOTHING IS GREATER THAN THE power of love that crosses all boundaries, and nothing is more disheartening than the power of hate that builds all boundaries."

My mother told us stories of my father being her knight in shining armor. When she would read us bedtime stories, I would ask her if I would find my knight. My father was the love of my mother's life. They were born one day apart under different circumstances. He was born into a poor family in a modest abode in a village on the outskirts of Benin. The following day my mother was born with fanfare into royalty and wealth in Benin City. The contrast of their birth did not change their destiny, they married thirty years later in London. Despite coming from an advantaged background, my mother was ready to give it all up and go into an unknown world with him. Her family, feeling she would not be able to cope, was worried for her but my mother was determined to be with him and vice versa.

Her father sent her to England to study nursing and midwifery. He thought if it were a passing phase she would forget my father while studying there. My mother refused to marry anyone else and they constantly wrote letters to each other. It took months for letters to get back and forth then. She encouraged my father to get a scholarship and meet her in England. My father, being a brilliant student, was able to get one. He connected with my mother, and the rest is history. They loved each other dearly and shared a deep bond.

For me now, time seemed to pass very slowly. The days stretched out and the nights were even longer. Maybe it was because we were not having fun. The atmosphere was tense. It seemed as if no one was coming to rescue Benin from captivity. My mother continued to show such gallantry as she protected us. We had heard no news about my father and siblings who had escaped. My mother concealed whatever anxiety she might have had as she focused on ensuring we were safe. As soon as we woke up in the morning she would turn on the radio and would leave it on in the background till we slept at night. I think she probably left the one in her bedroom on all night at a reduced volume.

This day seemed like it would be like any other day when we woke up. We had breakfast as usual. My cousin, the informant, came round to give us whatever information he had gathered. My mother fed him breakfast and, after he left, taught lessons with us focused on mathematics and English. After lunch we had siesta. Even if we could not sleep we had to be on our beds and rest for about an hour. As we lay there we could hear the radio in the hallway. All of a sudden we heard my father's voice bellowing out of it. My younger sister shouted "Daddy." I jumped out of bed to see if my mother was listening as well. My younger sister kept saying "Daddy is safe." We could hardly believe our ears. The radio show was a record request one, where you could send a message to someone and then request the disc jockey to play a song for the person. In those days there were no CDs or MP3 players. There were records called LP's or long play. Disc jockeys, played these records professionally.

The song my father picked was an old classic, one my mother said they used to dance to at Hammersmith Palais in London soon after they married. Hammersmith Palais was a popular venue for ballroom dancing and entertainment. My father said the message was to his dear wife Dora. He wanted her to know he and the children were safe and they all missed us and loved us very much. We were all ecstatic and jumping for joy. This was the first time we had heard his voice since they escaped. It was my mother's birthday and that was the best present she could have gotten. Aunties and uncles started trooping in to tell us and wanted to know if we, too, had heard the message. My father's greeting on the radio was so powerful; it had crossed so many boundaries and miles of war to get to us. We had been given a bright ray of hope and joy.

I thought nothing could take away the joy of hearing my father's voice on the radio. We were told we could go out and play. As we played in the garden, all of a sudden we heard gunshots. I saw a man fall to the ground in front of our fence. I ran inside holding the twins. I did not know who this man was. All I knew was that he was gunned down, sprayed with bullets, his life cut short.

Later, my cousin the informant told us what happened. He said a man was betrayed by a neighbour he trusted with his life. No one could trust anyone; betrayal of trust was becoming the order of the day. The neighbours were tired of hiding him and asked him to go back to his home. On his way there, a Biafran soldier spotted him in his long robe and immediately suspected he was a northerner. Without asking questions he was shot.

There were indiscriminate killings of innocent civilians who were caught in the middle because of their ethnicity or professional position. A lot of times when people were killed by the Biafran soldiers their *rigor mortis* bodies were just left on the streets to rot. They were not buried and people were too afraid to even move their bodies in case they too became targets. People walked passed the bloated lifeless bodies of people whose faces were not even covered, while wild boars tugged at their rotting flesh. During the war, death seemed to have neither meaning nor dignity.

The situation began to feel more permanent, especially after we heard a broadcast by Major Okwonkwo, the Biafran Military Administrator, establishing "the republic of Benin." In the first part of his broadcast he tried to convince the people of Benin that he had the support of their Oba and senior chiefs. He also listed the grievances Biafrans had with the Federal government and their justification for seceding. He then also proclaimed the secession of the Mid-Western region too stating:

> I, Major Albert Nwazu Okonkwo, Military Administrator of the territory known as Mid-Western Nigeria including the air space, territorial waters and continental shelf, mindful of the powers vested in me under Decree No. 2/1967 of Mid-Western Nigeria and other subsequent decrees, do hereby declare the said territory of Mid-Western Nigeria as the Republic of Benin, autonomous and completely sovereign. The Republic of Benin will perform all functions of a sovereign state, make any laws, enter into any treaty with any other sovereign state, prosecute war against the enemy, make peace and agree to enter into association for common services with any Region of the former Federation of Nigeria. The Republic of Benin shall collaborate with the Republic of Biafra in all military matters. We shall honor all international treaties and obligations, support the OAU, and as soon as possible apply for membership in the United Nations.

CHAPTER FOURTEEN

Hopes dashed...they did not come for us

NIGERIA HAD BEEN A BRITISH colony. Upon Independence, it became a member of the British Commonwealth. Those Nigerians who could afford to, sent their children to English boarding schools. The educational system in Nigeria was modeled after the British one. More Nigerians went on vacation to the United Kingdom than to anywhere else. It felt familiar for Nigerians to be in England as most streets in Nigeria bore British rather than Nigerian or African names.

Nevertheless, the average Nigerian never really trusted British intentions during the Civil War. They did not expect too much from the British and felt their support for the Federal government during the war was more out of concern for their financial investments than for the well-being of the Nigerian people. How could Nigeria totally trust them? After all, the British had divided the country up in colonial times in such a way that there would be continuous antagonism between the peoples of the south and the north, antagonisms that finally erupted in the post-independence civil war I was now living through. The United States, on the other hand, was viewed as a great and powerful nation. The Soviet Union and America were the superpowers of the world. America was referred to as "God's own country." Nigerians believed all sort of myths about the U.S. and some people feared it.

The Peace Corps was an American organization created by President John F. Kennedy in 1961. In his Inaugural Address, Kennedy asked Americans to "ask not what your country can do for you, but what you can do for your country." Thousands of young Americans responded by volunteering to serve in the Peace Corps. Its mission was to provide teachers, community developers and other technical assistants to developing countries. The volunteers lived like their counterparts in the countries where they served and received the same salaries as they did. They were given extensive training in local languages. By the time they returned to the United States after two years of service, they became great champions of the countries in which they served. Volunteers served in both the cities and the villages. In Nigeria they served in all the Regions, especially the East and Mid-West, which included Benin. I overheard discussions that, as the war started, some of the Peace Corps volunteers in the Mid-West had been relocated to Benin and kept in a safe house.

Through the Peace Corps, America had deeply rooted itself into Nigeria, its volunteers understanding the people and the culture. They completely identified with the people with whom they served and appeared to view the war from either a Nigerian or Biafran perspective. Most Peace Corps volunteers in the North, West and Midwest supported the Federal Government. Those in the East identified with the Biafran cause. Volunteers who returned home after their service in the East spoke out publicly on behalf of the separatists. In 2010, former volunteer John Sherman (Nigeria/Biafra 1966–67), who was teaching in the eastern region, wrote this about the volunteers' evacuation during the Biafran war:

> "We were distraught at being evacuated, hundreds
> of us chain-smoking and sharing stories on the bare

floor in the cargo hold of a ship that took us from the war zone of the secessionist Republic of Biafra to the Nigerian capital, Lagos ('enemy territory,' we called it), and on to new assignments. Our students, fellow tutors, friends, neighbors, market women, and lorry drivers were all left behind to face the growing chaos and, later, the horror felt worldwide: the malnutrition and death that, for people of a certain age around the globe, immediately come to mind when they hear [the name]'Biafra.' I took this war personally."

Weeks stretched on and we children had developed a routine of home school, then playing in the garden for exercise and sunlight. Whenever we played outside, a nanny had to be with us to make sure it was safe, or else she would use her discretion and keep us in the house. My mother was always nearby watching us while listening to the radio. I remember playing in the garden on a particular day when I suddenly saw my cousin, the informant, come running into our compound excitedly. He said he had important news. The nanny hurriedly took us inside to make sure she did not miss what he had to say. She loved listening to my cousin's stories. He told my mother we should be hopeful that we would soon be liberated, that the Americans were coming to our rescue. My mother asked him why he thought that. She said if the Americans were coming it would be to evacuate their citizens. My mother did not share his enthusiasm but my cousin held firm to his belief. The nanny was very excited as well and assured us that the Americans would soon save us. My mother did not want to dash our hopes so she merely said we should not worry, that, whatever the case was, everything would be fine and we would be rescued. Once my mother said that, I felt reassured, but inside me I hoped the Americans were coming to save us. How exciting that story would be to tell at school, I thought. But, alas, our hopes were dashed. The Americans had not come for us.

A few days later, I was in the garden playing, when the informant came again and told us that the Americans had sent their Peace Corps director for Africa to evacuate the Peace Corps volunteers. He said the director passed by our street but only the Peace Corps volunteers were taken. We were left behind. I would learn years later that the Peace Corp director for Africa was the future American ambassador to Nigeria and my future husband - Walter Carrington.

CHAPTER FIFTEEN

Faiths conquering...prayers are heard

FAITH IS BELIEF IN THINGS not yet seen. As time drags on, faith begins to wane. If it were something beyond the "now," why did the people have faith that Benin would be liberated from the Biafrans? The rich, the poor, Christians, Muslims and even traditional spiritualists were all praying that Benin would be liberated soon. At home my mother continued to lead evening prayers as my father had done every night before he escaped. We, including the nannies, would gather in the hallway, sit around the dining table and read the Bible before prayers. Everyday my mother made us recite the Lord's Prayer. Sometimes we would all declaim it together or she would ask one of us to deliver it from memory.

One day it was my turn to recite the Lord's Prayer. When I got to the end and said "Amen," I suddenly realized that, while I had committed the prayer to memory, I really did not know what it meant. I asked my mother some questions and she began to explain. She said every day that our needs were met, it was God giving us our daily bread and other blessings. She said God forgave us when we did naughty things so we had to forgive people when they did wrong things to us. I asked her if that meant we had to forgive the soldiers who put us in captivity. She told me that God wanted us always to be forgiving. She went on in depth. It was as

if I had set her off. My mother grew up a Baptist. She attended
Baptist missionary schools and at one time had wanted to be a
missionary. She worshiped at Baptist churches but started going to
Anglican services when she married my father, who was a member
of the Church of England. Yet, deep down, my mother remained
a Baptist. In the moment, her evangelical spirit broke through her
acquired Anglican reserve.

I have grown to share my mother's love of the Book of Psalms
and especially Psalm 23, which she would often have us recite. While
there is a psalm for every season, the 23rd was especially appropriate
in times of difficulty. Benin was in such a time. Another prayer we
would offer up as we knelt or lay in bed with our hands in a prayer
position was one called Matthew, Mark, Luke and John. It was an
English prayer, which many children who attended British schools
used to say:

> Matthew, Mark, Luke and John/
> Bless the bed that I lie on/
> Before I lay me down to sleep/
> I give my soul to Christ to keep/
> Four corners of my bed/
> Four angels there abide/
> One at the head and one at the feet. ...

I would stop before saying the last verse because of its emphasis
upon death. All around us there were too many fatalities caused
by war. That verse, which I had never thought much about before,
now seemed too disturbing and depressing for a child. After I told
my mother how fearful it made me, she no longer had us recite it.

The Edo people continued to render prayers and traditional
sacrifices entreating for release from captivity. Still, some began
to lose faith and felt we should just accept that we were going
to remain a part of Biafra. That was not something others were

ready to agree to for many reasons, including the fact that it would mean that they would be separated from family members who lived elsewhere in the country. We continued to believe that God has a way of answering prayers when his people are becoming faint and weary. Those in Benin were exhausted. When, they wondered, would their Lord deliver them?

One morning, to everyone's surprise, we awoke to the news that the Biafrans had been driven out. The long nightmare was over. It was September 20, 1967 and the Federal troops under the command of Major Murtala Muhammed had recaptured Benin.[17] I remember so many of my aunties running to our house, shouting in jubilation. It seems like only yesterday but it was, in fact, several decades ago. The atmosphere was like a carnival. They came smiling; some had run out of their houses forgetting to put on their shoes, their voices hoarse from shouting. They were thanking God in Edo singing "Ikponwonsa," which means I thank God, "Osamagbe" - God is good, and "Osaro"-there is a God. There was dancing and chanting up and down the street.

The Federal soldiers were driving through the streets in military trucks telling the people to come out and feel free. They had liberated Benin. We heard from the radio that the Nigerian government troops had surprised the rebels and overpowered them. The Biafran military had withdrawn. Those who were still in the barracks had taken off their uniforms and were trying to merge with the native Benin people to avoid capture.

My mother told us God had heard our prayers. We would soon be able to go to Lagos to be reunited with our family. I asked if we could go the next day, but she said we had to wait a bit to make sure the roads were safe. She also wanted to be reassured

---

17 Murtala as General Officer Commanding (GOC) the second division of the Nigerian army was given the task of recapturing the Midwest. He commandeered resources, vehicles and officers from the first division and incorporated them into a bigger and more forceful second division that was able to strategically recapture Benin and some other parts of the Midwest from the unprepared Biafrans.

that the situation in Benin was settled and secure. She said she would organize with some other families that also wanted to travel to Lagos so we could travel in a convoy.

My mother smiled and kissed us one by one. She brought out drinks for the guests that were streaming in. An elderly uncle told her to bring out a bottle of gin. When she brought it, he opened it and poured libations on the ground in front of the house in a true Benin tradition and thanked our ancestors for seeing us through captivity. The prayers of the Benin people had been heard, their faith in God had been rewarded.

CHAPTER SIXTEEN

*Humanity at its Worst and Best... 'I
am not who they say I am'*

INITIALLY, THE AIR OF FREEDOM seemed so fresh. Civilians were ecstatic to see the Federal soldiers and welcomed them with food, cheers and smiles. People jubilated on the streets, sharing the deep emotion of freedom. Market women slashed the prices of their food. The Federal troops were everywhere. They set up checkpoints and when they found Biafran troops they killed them. The Federal troops declared it a crime to hide rebel soldiers, the same way the Biafrans had earlier said it was crime to hide the Federal troops. As well, again there was mass killing of innocent civilians, but this time the Igbo. Their bodies would usually be dumped in a tipper trailer and buried in mass graves. It was déjà vu and such a sad loss of life.

I had never known what was behind the tall brick wall at the rear of our house. One day I saw the nannies climbing a table in the veranda and looking over it. They were squealing and wailing, so I climbed the table as well and got on my toes to see what was going on. As I looked I saw mass graves had been dug and truckloads of dead bodies were being dumped into them. When my mother found out we had been looking over the wall she forbade us from ever doing that again. It was too late. I could never forget what I had seen. The air around us was befouled with the stench of death.

The airwaves reminded us continually that it was a crime to house the Biafran soldiers or help them escape. The search, however, went beyond the soldiers. All Igbo were to report to military bases to prove they were not members of the Biafran army. People who helped the Igbo escape or hid them did so at their own peril. Suddenly, those Igbo who were settlers in Benin and had been trading there for years felt vulnerable. Their shops and stalls were looted and they were exposed by their neighbours. They, too, were trying to escape.

People began to take the law into their own hands, hunting Igbo people down and killing or maiming them. One afternoon my siblings and I were playing in the living room of our house, which faced onto the front garden and the street. Again, there was pandemonium on the street. I looked out through a window. Apparently an Igbo man was running from the federal soldiers. A mob cornered him right by the gate of our house. The man denied his ethnicity, swearing he was neither Igbo nor a Biafran soldier. The mob shouted back "He is Igbo, a Biafran soldier, kill him, kill him, *kill am, kill am.*" The man put his hand on his head saying, "I am not who they say I am, *I no be who dey say I be. I swear to God.*" His last word betrayed him when he said *"Chineke,"* which is the Igbo word for God. The next thing I saw was the man gunned down.

I continued to look out at the large fruit tree whose branches spread way beyond the perimeter of the wall. It provided shade on the street where weary souls tended to take refuge from the scorching sun and raging heat. Now it seemed it was providing refuge for dying souls. That memory and others of mob action and mob madness are forever imprinted in my mind.

The liberation of some became the oppression of others. There was so much looting that the Federal troops finally declared it a crime for civilians to loot any of the vacant houses or shops belonging to the Igbo. Soldiers went from house to house looking for looters and stolen property. Robbers became frightened and began burning their ill-gotten loot.

In addition to manning the checkpoints, the Federal troops were plying the roads. As they passed, people would shout "One Nigeria" and hail them for liberating Benin. The soldiers would return the cheers. One day our cousin, the informant, came to our house and told my mother to make sure we all knew that when we were stopped at checkpoints to greet the soldiers with "One Nigeria," the solidarity phrase. Our cousin had my younger siblings and me practice saying it. My younger brother had lost his two front teeth, so when he tried to say "One Nigeria" it sounded like he was saying "Fun Negeeria." He would then laugh out loud, revealing his missing front teeth.

It was so good to have laughter in the house again. I hugged my little brother tight. It suddenly occurred to me that no one had asked him if the tooth fairy had visited him when he lost his teeth. We had all been otherwise preoccupied during the Biafran occupation. I asked him what he did with his teeth when they fell out. He said he had kept them and was taking them back to Lagos to put under his pillow at the house there. He said he did not put them under his pillow at the house in Benin because he felt the tooth fairy would not come to a war zone. He said, "Fairies are all about peace, love and good things." I told him he was a very smart boy and I was sure the tooth fairy would give him extra money for not expecting a visit when Benin was occupied. I told him fairies don't believe in captivity. They want people to be free.

CHAPTER SEVENTEEN

The Reunion...never leave me again

THE FEW TELEPHONE LANDLINES THAT existed in Benin were reconnected. Although they behaved erratically, sometimes calls were able to get through to Lagos using the operator. Only local calls within Benin could (occasionally) be dialed directly. All calls to outside numbers had to be dialed through an operator who sometimes would not be able to hook up the call immediately. The operator would dial back when a connection was available.

My mother tried several times to call my father but she was only able to get through a couple of times. The first time was such a joyous occasion. We were all so excited to hear each other's voices. We had so many questions to ask and so much to tell. In those days when the operators dialed a call for you, they usually eavesdropped so you could never really have a private conversation. They would sometimes ask you to wind up your call because you had stayed on too long. I wondered how the length of time a person stayed on a phone was their business, but I later found out they had limited switch board connections and had to time people.

This day, even though they were inundated with people trying to make calls, they did not ask us to wind up, they did not interfere, and we spoke for what seemed to be hours. The phone boxes then were big and heavy. The color of our phone was black and had a dial pad on it. There was no way to put the phone on speaker so we could all listen at once and talk to my father at the same time. The phone was not portable and was fixed in one place. We all waited eagerly for our turn to speak. I had tears of joy in my eyes to be able to talk to my father again.

Finally, we traveled back to Lagos by road to our reunion. We went in a convoy of four cars with two other families who also lived in Lagos. My mother's car was third in the procession. She had hired a driver to drive my father's car back. His car brought up the rear of the convoy. There were several checkpoints on the way and still a lot of Federal troops plying the roads. However the journey was uneventful. When cars travelled together then, there were no cell phones to communicate. If one of the drivers behind the first car wanted to stop, its driver would put on a turn signal *(trafickator)*. The driver immediately in front would do the same and so on, till the lead car would see the signal of the vehicle immediately behind it and also stop. All cars would wait for the ones behind them to catch up until the procession was complete again. Then, the journey would continue.

My mother told our driver, Taiwo, to stop the car so she could buy food from the road side village women who had plantain heads, snails, yam tubers and fruits laid out on mats by the road. Because their farms were nearby and they had no transportation costs, their prices were very low. My mother always had her housewifely duties at the back of her mind and was thinking of the different dishes she would prepare for our reunion supper. For my part, I just wanted to get back as quickly as possible and see my father. Once we got to Shagamu town I was excited because I knew we were almost in Lagos. I was jumping up and down my seat as my fidgety self, returned. My mother had to ask me to sit still.

We finally got to Ikorodu on the outskirts of Lagos, then to Yaba and the Carter Bridge, which we crossed onto Lagos Island. I could barely wait. I had so much to tell my father. I had missed sitting on his right side at the dinner table and telling him everything that was going on. I felt I had discharged my duty very well by defending my younger siblings. I reminded them not to forget to tell our father how well I had looked after them. My younger brother had wrapped his teeth in a handkerchief and held on to them throughout the trip. He was looking forward to the tooth fairy finally paying him a visit. No one slept on the journey. It was as if we were taking in everything.

As we drove down our street and into our compound in Ikoyi, Taiwo blew the horn of the Opel Kapitän car several times. It was such a familiar reassuring sound. It was good to be back home. We saw everyone running out to welcome us, my father and siblings, the domestic staff and Taiwo's wife and child. Taiwo had been separated from his wife and daughter Sumbo throughout the ordeal. He ran and picked up his little girl, and then hugged his wife. She knelt to greet him as she usually did. My father went up to Taiwo and shook his hand and thanked him for driving us back safely. He asked him to take some time off to spend with his family. My parents hugged each other and then each went to the children from whom they had been separated. My mother was dancing with excitement. I was so happy to see my father and asked him never to leave me again. He smiled hugged me and said he would not. He was a constant figure in my life until the day he died. Even now, I feel his presence.

CHAPTER EIGHTEEN

The countdown…the war comes to an end

NOW THAT WE WERE SAFELY in Lagos the Biafran war seemed far away to me, but it was constantly at the back of my mind. Lagos was returning to normal. Although it took a couple of years, there were increasing signs the war was coming to an end as time elapsed.

The Federal troops continued to advance towards the East. During the war we heard stories about a feared and gallant Federal commander, Brigadier General Benjamin Adekunle, who led his troops with great determination. Adekunle the General Officer Commanding (GOC), Third Marine Commando Division (3MCD), had amongst his top commanders Lt. Col. Godwin Alabi-Isama and Lt.Col. Alani Akinrinade. The soldiers under his command were called Adekunle's Boys. I would listen to people as they extolled him. Our domestic staffs were always excited to tell us about the hero they fondly called "The Black Scorpion." They said Adekunle had liberated many places the Biafrans had captured. In the Midwest, amongst the towns he took control of or liberated were Aladima, Burutu, Escravos, Koko, Owa, Orerokpe, Sapele, Ughelli, Umutu, Urhonigbe and Warri. Our nannies told us that if he continued to defeat the rebels at that pace, the war would soon come to an end. He had attained a large following of fans.

John de St. Jorre, a journalist for the British newspaper *The Observer*, later wrote about Adekunle, "The 'Black Scorpion', Colonel Benjamin Adekunle, of the Third Marine Commando Division [was] Nigeria's most successful and controversial field commander to emerge during the war." Because he believed that winning the war justified the means he used, Adekunle sometimes employed methods that were seen as brutal, such as blocking humanitarian aid and taking very few prisoners. He was later relieved of his post as commander of the Third Marine Commando Division (3MCD) when his successive spell of capturing back Biafran territory came to a halt.

Unfortunately, the Federal government's continued blockade of food and humanitarian aid as well as arms to Biafra was causing a huge humanitarian crisis. Because the Igbo could not import food, innocent children starved and died. After a time, the will and strength of the Biafran people were weakened. The French Red Cross, sympathetic to the humanitarian plight in the East, was helping with relief centers, treating the injured and sick, and especially aiding the starving children suffering from Kwashiorkor (protein deficient malnutrition). I remember that whenever we wasted food my parents would remind us that the children trapped in the Biafran war zones were starving. I felt for them, but didn't know how eating up all my food would help them.

The Federal troops became more aggressive as they were able to attack the Biafrans from different sides, using both commando and infantry divisions. Colonel Olusegun Obasanjo succeeded Adekunle as leader of the 3rd Marine commando unit. The offensive that finally brought the war to an end began on January 7, 1970 and continued as Igbo towns fell one by one. St. Jorre wrote, "The crucial Federal breakthrough had occurred as far back as Christmas when the 3rd Marine commando had linked up with the 1st Division in Umuahia, isolating the important food producing salient of Arochukwu to the east and cutting Biafra in two."

On January 12, 1970, Major General Phillip Effiong, a senior member of the Biafran army to whom Ojukwu handed over power before fleeing his breakaway state, made an announcement over Radio Biafra asking his military to lay down their arms. The next day General Effiong made the official formal surrender to the Nigerian Head of State, General Gowon.

CHAPTER NINETEEN

Education and Ethnic tolerance

I HAD GRADUATED FROM ELEMENTARY SCHOOL. After briefly attending Queen's School, a secondary school in Ibadan, in 1970 my parents transferred me to a school in Lagos. I was now a boarder at Queens College, the premier girl's secondary school, which had been founded in 1927.[18] Sylvia Leith Ross was the Lady Superintendent for education and secretary of the board of education in 1927. She had been involved in the establishment of the college. Its motto was "Pass on the torch."

When I was at Queen's College it was situated on a large piece of land at Yaba, Lagos, which housed both the classrooms and the dormitories. The principal was Mrs. Coker, nicknamed "Cokey" by the students. Her house stood opposite the main gate, giving her a vantage point from which to view all that was happening on the school campus. She often strolled into the school compound in the evenings to check on things or catch people unawares. The gate was manned by security guards who required students and guests to sign in and out. Behind the gates students were meant to feel secure and safe from the war. Boarders were allowed out only

18 Sylvia Leith-Ross, Stepping Stones: Memoirs of Colonial Nigeria, 1907-1960, Pg 88, Peter Owen Publishers
Queen's College was the first Government secondary school for girls. Its first principal was Faith Words-worth (later Mrs. Tolfree)

with a special "exeat slip." Some of the seniors, however, used to sneak out. If they got caught doing so, the principal expelled them. Down the driveway from the gate on the left was the assembly hall. There, the school anthem, "Pass on the torch," written by Miss Dorothy Peel and its music composed by Mr. Woodham, was always sung at the end of term. It was a poignant anthem with a deep, inspiring and relevant meaning. I loved all of the four stanzas of the song, especially the last stanza, which was significant not just to us students but to the country as a whole. It was an anthem I proudly loved to sing.

Queen's College Logo

"Pass on the torch still brightly gleaming,
Pass on the hopes, the earnest dreaming
To those who follow close at hand.
Pass on the thoughts, the skills, the learning;
Pass on the secret in most yearning
That they may build where we have planned.

Pass on the songs, pass on the laughter,
Pass on the joy that others after
May tread more lightly on their way.
Pass on the faith that naught can alter,
Pass on the strength lest they should falter
In hours of stress some future day.

Pass on the firm determination

To guide a later generation
By gentle influence in the home.
Pass on the health, the youthful vigour,
Pass on the love that can transfigure,
The darkest hours that yet may come.

Pass on the torch, the cry inspiring
Unites us here in hopes untiring,
In bonds no future years can sever.
We forward press not backward turning;
That this our torch more brightly burning
May yet pass on and on forever."

QUEENS COLLEGE YABA 1970

Mrs. Coker's office was next to the assembly hall and it was not a place students liked to visit. Anyone waiting outside it was usually in trouble. Behind the assembly hall was a small quadrangle where students and parents used to sit on benches on visiting Sundays. On one side of the quadrangle was a corridor that led to the rest of the school, which lay around a large courtyard. On its sides lay the classroom block, the dining room and the two dormitory blocks, one of which had the music room and science laboratory underneath. The school had six forms. Each was divided into two arms, Q and S.

The boarding school students were divided amongst the

dormitory block according to their schoolhouse, which bore names from the four regions. The school's concept of deriving house names from all the different regions of the country further underscored the school's ideals of national unity and ethnic tolerance. These ideals were especially significant as Nigeria was now trying to heal from the division of the civil war. There was yellow colored Obi house, whose name was derived from the Eastern Region; red Danfodio house from the Northern Region; green Emotan house from the Mid-West; and blue Obasa house from the West. Students were randomly assigned, ensuring that a significant number of them would end up in houses bearing names of people from regions other than their own. I, for instance, although from the Mid-Western Region, was assigned to Obi house. The liveliest competition between the dormitories was in inter-house sports. On sports day, Danfodio and Obi house usually excelled. The rivalry between these two houses on the field mirrored the rivalry between the regions that fought a civil war.

Students sometimes possessed forbidden items, which they referred to as contraband. The most common thing smuggled in was cooked food, since some students had a preference for their own ethnic dishes. Many Hausa girls usually brought their ethnic delicacy *Kilishi*, made out of dried thinly sliced pieces of meat roasted with a spicy peanut sauce. If the housemistress caught a student with contraband, it was confiscated and, if the wrongdoer was unlucky, she got sent to the principal's office. I think we were allowed transistor radios. I had a tiny red one and would listen to it whenever I could. I had not forgotten what my father had told my mother about listening to the radio to keep abreast of the war. I followed the countdown as each day it was announced which Igbo town in the east had fallen to the federal troops. I can't remember the announcements in great detail, but I have never forgotten that on January 13, 1970 the Biafran war finally ended. Finally, I felt a measure of peace within.

CHAPTER TWENTY

The rhapsody of peace...the healing begins

THE WAR WAS OVER, BUT so much damage had been done physically, emotionally and structurally in the Eastern Region. Pictures of starving Biafran children were shown all over the world. A leading charitable organization, Doctors without Borders, was later founded by a group of physicians some of whom had worked in Biafra providing relief during the crisis. Physicians went to the East to render medical services to the demoralized population who felt they had sacrificed so much and lost so many of their people in a failed effort to secede. Some estimates placed the number of people killed during the war at about two million, most of whom were Biafran soldiers during battle, as well as Igbo children from Kwashiorkor disease.

Although Lt. Col Ojukwu had flown out of Biafra a few days before the surrender, the Igbo people still felt he was a great leader, but now they had to accept defeat and merge back with Nigeria. They were not sure how they would be received. Their homeland had taken the brunt of the war. Much of the infrastructure had been laid waste by bombing, including the Niger Bridge which joined the Eastern Region to the rest of the country. Homes and public buildings had been destroyed. The Federal Government launched a reconstruction effort.

During the war, the children in the East had not been able to go to school outside their Region, and there were few open schools. Home schooling was also very erratic. As a result, they were now several classes behind their former classmates in Lagos and elsewhere in the country. When they returned to school, they were placed in classes below their age. Some felt self-conscious because they looked much older than their classmates and found it difficult to adjust.

Nigeria had changed the country's currency during the war so the Igbo had lost whatever money they had in the old legal tender. The refugees and physically displaced had to be rehabilitated. Even though the Nigerian head of State, General Gowon, had tried to ease the pain of the war and welcome back the Igbo, it was difficult to erase the seeds that had been planted in children's minds during the years of conflict. Some still saw the Igbo only as Biafran rebels. Some of them were picked on and called names like "Rebel's child" or "Omo Biafra" - a Biafran child. As a matter of fact, these became terms that bullies often used as cruel taunts. During the war, the rebels had been portrayed as traitors who wanted to break Nigeria up. It takes time for wounds to heal, but this was a major lesion Nigeria had to mend in order to keep the nation as one.

General Gowon saved the situation. His post civil war policy of Rehabilitation, Reconstruction and Reconciliation was referred to as the 3Rs. There was a difficult road ahead in realizing a truly "One Nigeria." In declaring the war over, Gowon advised people to have sober reflections. He welcomed the Igbo back into Nigeria and his post war theme was: "No Victors, No Vanquished."

In his broadcast from Lagos, 15 January 1970 titled 'The Dawn of National Reconciliation' Gowon went down the painful history that led to the civil war and finally its end. But most importantly he wanted everyone to join together to build a nation of equality and national unity. He said,

On our side, we fought the war with great caution, not in anger or hatred, but always in the hope that common sense would prevail. Many times we sought a negotiated settlement, not out of weakness, but in order to minimize the problems of reintegration, reconciliation, and reconstruction. We knew that however the war ended, in the battlefield, or in the conference room, our brothers fighting under other colours must rejoin us and that we must together rebuild the nation anew.

For me, just the thought that the war was over was a huge relief. I did not have to worry about bombs, sirens, being separated from loved ones, or being under captivity. People had seen war and now they wanted to bask in the rhapsody of peace. So much had happened. I was no longer naïve about war.

From time to time, I still wondered about my Palestinian friend--where she was, what country she was in, and if her family had found a place at peace. Did war stop following her? I remember her apartment in South West Ikoyi overlooking the water. I remember the stairway I used to run up in excitement and anticipation of seeing her. I even remember details of her apartment, but I don't remember her name and I can't see her face. It is as if I can't get to that part of my subconscious where I buried that information. Maybe it is too painful to remember because that moment when she looked into my face and told me of a pending war was the moment my carefree innocence was shattered.

PART TWO

AN EPIC LOVE IN A WAR AGAINST DICTATORSHIP

CHAPTER TWENTY ONE

A Synopsis of the aftermath...things that followed

THE WAR HAD ENDED, MY family had been reunited. My parents forbade my siblings and me to talk about the war and our experiences. They believed it was best for us to forget. They were not psychologists and they felt they were protecting us. We obeyed them and buried the nightmare of the war deep in our subconscious. My father focused on us getting the best education and excelling. My two brothers became civil engineers, my eldest sister became a lawyer and the next two sisters a chartered accountant and linguist, respectively. I became a doctor and my other sister got degrees in both law and accounting.

It was not until years later, as an adult, that I learned the details of the hazardous escape the other half of my family had made. My eldest sister had kept a journal. The night they left with the guide, he drove them to a nearby town called Sapele, making sure to take all the back roads. They then travelled by land through the thick forest, led by a hunter with a lantern and a hunting rifle. They spent the night wandering through the snake-infested forest. Their group of about twenty five people consisted of children and adults from different walks of life with a few necessities trying to escape a raging war. The hunter safely navigated them through gunshots and fighting soldiers in the background. They got to

Sapele-riverside where he handed them over to a fisherman who owned a rickety boat. The boat looked more like a large canoe with an engine board attached to it. There were other groups of people by the riverbank that had also paid for the passage. In total, my sister said she counted about two hundred people. Surely the canoe was not meant to carry two hundred people, she thought, but it did, and no one dared to either complain or turn back. They all sat close together on the boat.

It would be about half a week before they would get to shore. The fisherman and his apprentice navigated through the narrow Niger delta creeks, trying to avoid the soldiers as they headed towards a shore town called Okitipupa. My sister said they passed some villages deep inside the creeks where the inhabitants were so far removed they did not even know there was a war going on. As they passed Koko village, they got fired at by Biafran soldiers who were trying to put bullet holes in the canoe to sink it. To no avail, the passengers waved white handkerchiefs and shouted "We are civilians." As it dawned on them that the Biafran soldiers were out to kill them, people began to scream and tried to rush to the furthest end of the canoe almost capsizing it. The passengers then begged the fisherman to surrender to the Biafran soldiers so their canoe would not be sunk. Apparently most of the passengers could not swim. The fisherman refused to surrender saying there was no guarantee they would not be killed by the Biafran soldiers since they were escapees. Through it all, there was a woman who held on to her precious chicken, fed and nurtured it, much to the annoyance of some of the escapees. There were quarrels and frayed nerves throughout the journey, but my siblings said my father was always the voice of reason and tried to maintain calm, warning everyone that their paramount objective should be to work together to ensure they all arrived in Lagos safely.

My older brother fell very ill on the latter part of the canoe trip. He started to shiver, had a high temperature and had probably caught malaria. My eldest sister said she had been trying to control herself throughout the trip, but, seeing our brother like that and fearing for his life, she broke down in tears and started screaming erratically. On the fourth day, they arrived on the Okitipupa shore from where they would continue the rest of the journey to Lagos by road. They were all tired and malnourished. Some of the children had malaria and were dehydrated, but everyone made it, except for the chicken.

The escapees waved white handkerchiefs in the air as they climbed out of the canoe and were surrounded by the villagers. They were advised that Benin was probably safer than there right now and maybe they should head back. Unbeknownst to the escapees, the Biafran troops had already advanced to Okitipupa on route to Lagos. The Federal troops were trying to prevent them from getting to the capital and had turned the village into a serious battleground. My sister said that by this time, my brother had gotten progressively worse and was in no position to travel back. He needed medical care. Returning was not an option my father was even considering. The principal of the local school was one of the people that came to the shoreline when the canoe arrived. On seeing my brother's state he came over to my father, introduced himself and offered to take them in until my brother was better and they could continue on their journey. He helped get medication for him and nursed him back to health.

The school principal was a Good Samaritan. He organized for a local taxi driver who knew the back roads through the villages and bushes to drive my father and siblings to Lagos. Each time they came across people, the taxi driver and my father would wave a white handkerchief. They did not venture near the major roads at all. When they finally did escape the war torn zone and arrived in Lagos, my father knew that the journey was too treacherous and unpredictable for the other half of the family ever to take. After my sister told me this story, we remembered my parents had said we should not recount our war experiences, so again we pushed them into our subconscious.

CHAPTER TWENTY TWO

A fate so compelling

DESPITE UNIFICATION EFFORTS AFTER THE civil war, Nigeria continued to struggle under Gowon, and distrust continued amongst its different ethnic groups. Gowon failed to keep his promise to return Nigeria to civilian rule in 1974. A year later, he was ousted by General Murtala Mohamed. Military coups became the order of the day. In 1976, Murtala was assassinated in a botched, bloody coup by Col Burka Suka Dimka. General Obasanjo, Murtala's chief of staff, became the military Head of State. After a new constitution was written in 1978 to ensure a return to civilian rule, Obasanjo held elections in 1979 and handed over power to the civilian winner, Alhaji Shehu Shagari, who became the president of the Second Republic, ending the string of successive military rulers since the Civil War. Shagari ran for a second term in 1983 and, after contested results decided by the Supreme Court ruling, Shagari was proclaimed the winner.

However, in December 1983 Major General Muhammadu Buhari toppled the Shagari regime, truncating the short-lived Second Republic. Nigeria again fell under military rule. Buhari declared a "war against indiscipline" (WAI) with serious consequences for corruption and indiscipline in any sector. He ruled Nigeria until August 1985.

In 1985, another military figure, General Ibrahim Babaginda staged a successful coup against Buhari. Babaginda prevented coup plotters from overthrowing him by executing his fellow coup plotters. He executed the first set in 1986, including his friend General Maman Vatsa and in 1990 another group led by Gideon Orkar.

As democratic change swept across other African countries, most Nigerians continued to yearn for the democracy that seemed to elude them. In 1990, Babaginda proclaimed a new constitution that would return the nation to civilian rule in two years. But his intentions seemed unclear. He annulled the 1992 electoral process, claiming it was flawed. After various revisions to the process, he allowed elections in 1993. However, before the presumed winner was announced, he annulled the 1993 presidential election despite their being labelled by observers as the free and fairest elections Nigeria had ever held.

The young American Peace Corps official who came to war-torn Benin to rescue the Peace Corps volunteers was Walter Carrington. He returned to Nigeria in 1993 as the United States Ambassador. A Harvard College and Law School graduate, Walter was the thirteenth American Ambassador to Nigeria since the United States embassy was established in Lagos on October 1, 1960. He presented his credentials on November 9, 1993 while Nigeria was again going through political turmoil. The military regime of General Ibrahim Babangida had annulled the June 12, 1993 elections which were deemed to be the freest and fairest elections the country had ever held. An interim government was put in place only to be replaced by another military dictatorship two weeks after Walter arrived.

Twenty five years earlier, when Walter came to Benin City to evacuate the Peace Corps volunteers, I was a child playing in my garden. Although our destinies would be intertwined, at that time we were oblivious of each other. We may have seen each other as I played in the garden and he picked up the volunteers. Who knows?

Now I was an adult, a medical doctor, and fate would throw us together again at Walter's first public engagement after presenting his credentials. The occasion was the Belgian National Day, the venue was the Belgian Ambassador's garden on Eleke Crescent (now renamed Walter Carrington Crescent). This time we were aware of each other's presence, but initially unaware that we had been in close proximity to each other once before.

People often ask me details of how I met my husband. It was November 15, 1993. I had no idea what destiny had in store for me that day. It was like any other busy day, juggling my business meetings for the promotional items company I ran, as well as my medical consultancy. It was a common practice in Nigeria for professionals to also run other non-related businesses on the side. I was about to head home when I suddenly remembered it was the Belgian King's Day and the Belgian Ambassador was hosting a reception at the embassy. I had intended to give myself enough time to change into a formal outfit at home. It was already six p.m. and the sun was setting. I knew there was not enough time to change because the evening traffic had started. Since I was wearing a smart business suit I decided I would go directly to the reception. It was important I attended as a show of support because the Belgian Ambassador and some of his staff were my medical clients.

At the reception I greeted the Belgian Ambassador and his wife in the receiving line, then made my way through the crowd. Later, when I was about to leave, I saw a gentleman standing before me as I was talking to the head of the Franco-Nigerian Chamber of Commerce. He introduced himself as Walter Carrington, the new American Ambassador, and said he arrived only a few weeks prior. I was introduced to him as Arese, a medical doctor who worked with some of the embassies and multinational companies. As I turned to leave, the American Ambassador said to me, "Since I came to Nigeria I have put on weight from the food. I need a doctor to help me with suggestions on a healthy diet here." He handed me his complimentary card with his detailed information, and asked if I would help him with that. I took the card and said I would. As is generally done, I then gave him my card in exchange.

I drove through the Lagos traffic home, satisfied that I had attended the reception. When I got home, as I usually did after any reception, I looked through my bag, took all the complimentary cards out and put them in a large bowl I kept at the side of my desk and forgot about them. I had a lot of cards in the bowl because I attended many diplomatic and business receptions. But as a rule I never contacted the people on the cards unless they contacted me. I felt that by refraining from making first contact one did not seem desperate for a favor, as diplomats often become overwhelmed by acquaintances asking them for visa favors. I found that I usually got invitations for other functions subsequently and then developed friendships. For example, I had developed nice friendships with some staff of the British Council and their families. We would plan fun weekends to the beach and shopping at the local markets for artifacts.

Two weeks later on Sunday, as I was preparing to go to the beach with my daughter and friends from the British Council, I got an invitation from the American Ambassador to attend a concert by Nina Simone at the embassy residence. The dispatch rider who delivered the invitation had refused to let my security guard sign for it but insisted that he had been instructed that I sign for the letter myself. My security guard relayed the message to me, so on my way out to the beach I signed for the invitation.

I had never heard of Nina Simone, so I really did not think I would attend. When I got to the beach, I told my friends about the invitation and they all went hysterical asking if they could go in place of me. At that moment, it occurred to me Nina Simone must be a big deal and I told everyone I had reconsidered. I would honor the invitation myself. Inquiring more about Nina Simone, I realized she was a famous jazz singer, a pianist and song writer.

Nina was known to be very emotional and erratic at times. She was also famous for being a civil rights activist and inspired a lot of young talent. Nina and her concert would be part of the series of events that led to my destiny.

The Ambassador's residence was situated in the quiet upscale suburb of Ikoyi on about five acres of land. A wall surrounded the whole premises, in the middle of which sat a uniquely shaped elongated two storey building. Two massive electronic black gates and security rams were at either end of the semicircular driveway. Security guards manned both ends. Half way down the drive way was the covered front porch that led to the entrance. Guests who had entry clearance were dropped off there.

A doorman dressed in a white uniform opened my car door. An embassy staff member ushered me in through a huge double doorway. As the oak doors were flung open, straight ahead of the lobby was an impressive stairway. The powder room was to the immediate right of the entrance in the lobby area. The sitting area had an open floor plan with high ceilings. To the left of the entrance was a formal sitting area with French doors that gave a bird's eye view of the garden and ocean. To the right of the entrance were two other sitting areas. The furnishing was classic and beautiful. Paintings adorned the walls. I was led through the formal sitting area to an open verandah with a grand piano in the center. It was placed there in preparation for the concert. The garden was expansive and all lit up. About two hundred people mingled around, with their drinks in one hand and hors d'oeuvres in the other at the pre-concert reception.

It was a cool breezy evening. I could smell the roses and other flowering plants that beautified the garden. The lawn was immaculate, well cared for and overlooked the calm sea. In the distance were a few canoes paddling by. On one extreme side of the lawn were tennis courts and on the other was the swimming pool, the pool house and a barbeque area. It was so picturesque.

The concert began with the Ambassador introducing Nina Simone. Her voice resonated through the air. Listening to Nina was euphoric. It was clear she was a master in her field. As guests left at the end of the concert, I went to Ambassador Carrington and thanked him for the invitation. He invited me to stay for an impromptu after-party indoors in the formal sitting room. He also asked I forget the formalities and call him by name. I told him I could not stay and needed to get home early. He said he would appreciate it if I graced the party briefly. I agreed to stay for five minutes. At the party I was introduced to Nina, and upon hearing that I was a doctor she explained to me that she forgot to bring her over the counter medication. She asked me if I could get it for her. I asked her how I should send it to her once I got it. Walter immediately said I should bring it to him and he would give it to her. At the after party Walter told me about himself and mentioned he was divorced.

Two days later, armed with Nina's medication, I called Walter and said I was going to drop Nina's medication with the guards at his residence. He told me not to do that and asked me over for dinner to deliver it personally to him. I gave him Nina's medication but politely turned down the dinner invitation because I was going out of town to visit my parents for Christmas vacation the next day. I agreed to take a rain check on the dinner invitation. I ended up not travelling the next day and Walter called to see if I had travelled and insisted since I had not, I should please come for dinner. I could not think up any excuse so I accepted.

It was a beautiful moonlit dinner for two set outdoors in the garden overlooking the sea. Everything seemed to stand still, even time, as we talked about different topics and debated various issues. We then went indoors to the formal sitting room for coffee and music. Walter proceeded to tell me the love story of how his next door neighbour the Dutch Ambassador and his American wife met.

The Dutch Ambassador had previously served as the Dutch

Consul General in America and was stationed in Houston, Texas. While there, he was watching television when on the news he saw a report of a terrible family car accident in which only a baby survived. The baby was shown on television being carried by a social worker as pleas were made for anyone who had information on the baby's relatives to come forward. The Dutch Ambassador was moved by the news report, but at the same time was attracted to the social worker. It was love at first sight. He asked his secretary to find out the name of the social worker. He then asked the social worker to be his date for a consul's ball he was about to attend. The social worker accepted the invitation and the rest is history. What led to their union was a tragic event, but out of a heartbreaking incident emerged a lasting and heartfelt love.

Walter told the story in such a romantic and emotional way that he brought tears to my eyes. I asked him if he believed in fairy tales and 'happily ever after,' to which he answered, yes. Men are not usually open about sensitive feelings, so his honesty was refreshing to me.

By the formal sitting area was the base of the staircase. On the wall by the base of the staircase was a striking painting by Alade Glover. Walter told me that very spot by the painting was significant to him. When he first visited Nigeria leading a group of students in a program called The Experiment in International Living they had taken a picture with the Consul General at the base of the staircase. Little did he know then, that he would become the Ambassador several years later and live in the very same house. In one of the rooms were his personal memorabilia. He showed me the paddle that he had used to initiate Martin Luther King, Jr. into his fraternity, Alpha Phi Alpha. Engraved on the paddle are the words: to Big Brother Wally from Martin Luther King. Walter sat on the sofa and I sat beside him. We listened to classical music and jazz. He told me how relaxing and pleasant it was being with me. He seemed so excited and happy. He held my hands as we later watched a video, *Mississippi Masala*.

The evening had been delightful. I had to leave because I was travelling by road to Benin City early the next morning to spend Christmas with my parents and extended family. It was a Christmas tradition. He then told me he had gotten an invitation to visit Benin in a couple of days and if it was okay with me, he would visit me at my parents' place while in Benin. I thought he was joking, so I said yes. His secretary called me up the next morning to ask for my contact information in Benin. The day after I arrived in Benin I got a brief call from his secretary saying, "Mr. Ambassador is on his way to Benin and will be visiting you."

I was flabbergasted. This was his first visit to Benin as the American Ambassador so it was important to show him great hospitality. I informed my parents about his visit. My father wondered why he was coming, so like a schoolgirl I began trying to explain. Thankfully my mother butted in reminding my father that I consult for some embassies and multinational companies. She said there was plenty to do in order to put together a welcome party for the Ambassador by that evening. That put an end to my father's interrogation.

My parents sent out invitations to uncles, aunties and special guests to attend a reception for the American Ambassador. Though it was impromptu, people were thrilled to come and meet him. America is referred to as "God's own country" in Nigeria and the ambassador was its representative. We organized traditional dancers as well as an abundance of delicious food and drinks. In one day, my parents put together a swell party. I jokingly told them if they wanted a retirement profession they would make great party planners. The Ambassador was delayed by his host but eventually arrived. It was a magnificent evening in which everyone enjoyed themselves. He got to meet my family, including my uncle who was the former Nigerian Ambassador to South Korea.

When the guests left, Walter asked to take a walk around the garden. My parent's home was on a large expanse of land in a newly developed residential area by the airport, called G.R.A (Government Residential Area). The compound was enclosed by a white wall. At one corner of the premises, there were two large white gates on either side of a semicircular driveway in front of the main house. Behind the house was a guest chalet by the swimming pool and two self-contained apartments for extended family members. My parents lived in the main house, which was a large white two-storey building. The compound was built after the Nigerian civil war. My parents wanted us to leave the memory of our war experience behind in the former house we had lived in then. My father took pride in the well kept sprawling lawn. The *Axonopus compressus* grass was mowed regularly. The back of one end of the lawn had an orchard with almond, mango and banana trees. Opposite the orchard was the gazebo. My mother said it was getting dark so she gave us flashlights. She told us to watch out for reptiles such as garden snakes. There were hardly any mosquitoes that night as we walked towards the gazebo, holding hands.

That night, we had our first passionate kiss at the gazebo in my parent's garden. We'd both come a long way from the time when Walter evacuated the Peace Corps volunteers and I was a child under captivity in Benin. Still, I felt like a little schoolgirl sneaking a kiss behind her parent's back. I looked into his eyes. From that moment I knew he had won my heart and I had found my soul mate. I knew this time he would not leave me behind.

CHAPTER TWENTY THREE

The processes...Diplomatic clearance, our
union, my naturalization and more

AFTER THE VISIT TO BENIN, Walter and I became an item.
I definitely wanted to keep it quiet, especially from the
press, which would be all over me. I decided we should
avoid being seen together in public, so even when we attended
diplomatic functions we arrived and left at different times. I
became an artful dodger and avoided the press getting a hint of our
relationship until we got engaged.

Most of the diplomatic functions I attended were the national
days of the various countries. The guests were nationals of that
country living in Nigeria, diplomats from other countries, Nigerian
external affairs officials and Nigerians from various walks of life.
The guests were always smartly dressed. Some wore their traditional
attire. Stewards in white uniforms passed around drinks and hors
d'oeuvres. I successfully evaded the press until a function at the
Indian High Commission at which Walter was giving a speech on
Gandhi. We decided to ride in the same car. The press was waiting
to take pictures as we stepped out of the car. Later that evening a
picture of us with other guests was taken. The next day the picture
appeared in the newspapers and the press began to ask questions.

Some months into our relationship, we travelled to the United

States. Walter wanted me to meet his sister in Boston and his stepmother in California. I was not well acquainted with America although I had been there before on vacation. Walter's sister Marylyn lined up interesting events for us and made sure we enjoyed our stay in Boston. After Boston, we went to Washington D.C. where Walter had some briefings at the State Department. I met senators, congressmen and other diplomats. One of Walter's friends had a dinner party for us. Amongst the guests were other diplomats, some senators and congressmen. For dinner, the guests were divided into two rooms. I was put in a separate room from Walter and was seated beside a congressman and a former senator. The host was also at my table. During dinner, different political topics were discussed and I was asked a lot of questions. The discussions were lively and I contributed heartily. I almost felt as if I was being "vetted" by the guests. After dinner, the entire group moved to the same room for dessert and coffee. I overheard a number of the people who were seated in my dining area, including the host, tell Walter; he was a lucky man. I guess I passed the test.

We left Washington D.C and flew to California. The last time I had visited the west coast I went to Disneyland. This time it was to make a quick visit to meet Walter's ailing stepmother in California. I was glad to have met her; she was very nice and obviously very fond of Walter. She had been a maid and personal assistant to a number of Hollywood stars when she was younger. She had written a book about them and the time she spent with them. She gave us the book and said we may want to publish it someday. We spent a couple of days with her and then the rest of the time at the Claremont resort.

I had studied about the Golden Gate Bridge at school in Nigeria. The marvel and beauty of the suspension bridge in California made it a tourist attraction. My father, who was an engineer, had told me it was one of the great engineering feats of the modern world. I often daydreamed about visiting the bridge. When I first met Walter, I had mentioned my admiration of the bridge and that I wanted to visit it. He must have kept that tucked away in his mind because he proposed to me one evening at Vista Point of the Golden Gate Bridge, San Francisco's lights glittering in the distance. He held my hand then slipped an engagement ring unto my finger and asked me to marry him. I said Yes!!! It was magical.

The evening we decided to announce the engagement, Walter had a private dinner for my parents and siblings. After dinner, he asked my father for my hand in marriage. My father drilled him and jokingly said, in the Benin traditional manner, that Walter was supposed to present cows, goats, cowries and a dowry to the family when asking for the hand of a princess in Benin. He said since he felt Walter was a good man and would take care of me, he would accept his request and excuse him from the traditional presentations. My father congratulated us and in the traditional way placed me on Walter's lap and prayed for our union. He thanked Walter for his devotion to ensuring human rights and democracy in Nigeria and asked him to continue to support the people.

Having gotten the blessing to marry me from my father, as the American Ambassador, Walter also had to get clearance from the State Department to marry me. His position is regarded as a sensitive one because it allows access to worldwide classified cables from the State Department. Before an ambassador can marry someone from a host country, the prospective spouse must jump a hurdle of clearances. I guess they have to make sure a spy is not trying to infiltrate.

Walter was counseled about the consequences to his job if during my background security checks any issues arose. I began the various checks to obtain the clearances needed to marry Walter. I had to complete a mountain of paperwork, literally remembering what I had done, to whom I had spoken and my involvement or non-involvement with certain countries. There was the police background check to be passed, Federal Bureau of Investigation (FBI) clearance and medical clearance to be obtained, amongst others. It was a long and arduous process but Walter's secretary, Sandra Slaughter, was very helpful. At the end of the process, which took several months, Walter received a cable from the State Department, Washington D.C. congratulating him that I had passed all the different clearances. Walter and I now had approval from State Department to marry.

The month of February is significant in American history. Abraham Lincoln, arguably one of America's greatest presidents was born in February. In America, February is also Black History Month and President's Day also occurs in that month. Also with Valentine's Day, love is in the air in February. Walter and I chose February 18th for our wedding.

With the date sorted out, we decided to elope and have a quiet wedding. We both felt it would be difficult to limit the number of guests to a public event. Very Important Personalities (VIPs), government functionaries, business Chief Executive Officers (CEOs) and my relatives would all expect invitations. I remember shortly after we had gotten married, a CEO of a company came up to us at a function and congratulated us. He said he got our wedding invitation but was out of the country so could not attend. He assumed we married in the country and because he was a CEO and a VIP he must have gotten an invitation. He did not realize we had eloped and never sent out any invitations.

Our wedding was in Cotonou in the Republic of Benin (formerly country of Dahomey). It was an unconventional ceremony and an intimate affair. The only guests were my younger sister, Walter's secretary Sandra, his Deputy Chief of Mission (DCM) secretary Niceta, his embassy chauffeur Tiko who drove us down, Ambassador Ruth Davis, U.S. Ambassador to Benin Republic and Gerry Olson, the Canadian High commissioner to Nigeria. My daughter was my flower girl.

Our love story is best told by both of us. In his own words at our wedding reception, this is what Walter said about how our first meeting blossomed into a union:

> A new Ambassador is almost a non-person outside of his own embassy. Until his or her credentials are presented to the Head of State, protocol calls for abstaining from appearing at diplomatic events. Sometimes the waiting period can be long. In my case it was brief. The Interim National Government (ING) expedited the process and my credentials were accepted within a week of my arrival. My first appearance occurred a few days later at the National Day reception hosted by the Belgian ambassador. The grounds were filled with people whom I did not yet know. As I stood talking to a French businessman, my eyes wandered and across that crowded garden I saw a woman of breathtaking beauty. I asked the man with whom I was exchanging pleasantries who she was. "Dr. Arese Ukpoma," he replied. She had a private practice but also served as the physician for some of the embassies and multinational companies. I asked him if he would introduce me.
>
> She seemed not at all impressed by my title. But I was deeply impressed by her. She apologized that she was about to leave to pick up her young daughter. I knew I had to come up with a credible excuse to see her again. With only the slightest bit of exaggeration I told her that since coming to Lagos, I was having a difficult time staying on a healthy diet. Perhaps she could recommend to me which of the local foods would be least likely to harm my diet if taken in moderation. She smiled and diplomatically assured

me that she would. We exchanged cards and then she took her leave.

I thought over the next few days of a suitable embassy function I might invite her to attend. And then as if by miracle, my favorite singer turned up in Lagos. Turned up without a visa! After all she was Nina Simone and did not feel she needed an entry permit to visit a country on the mother land. The officials at Murtala Muhammed airport did not agree. They were about to put her on the next flight out of Nigeria when an official of the American Embassy who was there to meet someone else recognised her and intervened on her behalf. They agreed to let her in but insisted on holding her passport. The next evening an angry diva appeared at my residence just as I was preparing to leave to attend some diplomatic functions. After an hour or so I got her to calm down and promised that I would see if her passport could be returned to her. I asked and she agreed to sing at a special reception I would throw in her honor. On the list of invitees I included Dr. Arese Ukpoma, whose business card I had kept specially. She attended the performance and stayed for a small private reception.

Nina Simone, it turned out was a bit of a hypochondriac. She was anxious to get some prescriptions filled. Arese agreed to help her and then asked Nina what was the best way to get them to her. I immediately said that she should bring them to me and I would see that Ms. Simone got them. Arese agreed and said that she would call me when they were ready. When she called I suggested that she bring them by the residence and stay for an informal dinner. We set a date and then she called again to say that she would not be able to come on that day because she and some of her relatives would be traveling to the family home in Benin for the holidays. Luckily, her trip was postponed and she said she would be able to come by as previously agreed.

We had an intimate dinner for two and watched the movie *"Mississippi Masala."* Many couples have a favorite song connected with their first date; we have that Denzel Washington film. And we have the whole Nina Simone playbook. Never had she been so effective an enabler of love as she was on that visit to Nigeria.

I was invited by a businessman to visit him in Benin. When my secretary informed Arese I was going to be in her home town and would be visiting her, she arranged for her father to throw a reception at their house. It was a spectacular affair with traditional dancers and lots of good food.

Back in Lagos, after returning from Benin, our love began to blossom. When I asked her to marry me, her father exempted me from fulfilling the traditional requirement of offering up cows and other goods in return for her hand. There was no such exemption from State Department, thus began the long period of bureaucratic red tape. For an American ambassador to marry a foreigner there are many hurdles and security background checks to surmount. When that was all done, we had to plan the wedding. To have had it in Nigeria might have caused all sorts of problems. We risked offending more people that we did not invite than pleasing those few whom we did. We feared being showered with extravagant gifts most of which under U.S. government regulations, I as a serving ambassador could not accept. So, reluctantly we decided to elope.

My good friend Ruth Davis, the American Ambassador to Benin, agreed to help us exchange our vows here. As those present at the wedding ceremony witnessed it was the Mayor of one of Cotonou's *arrondisments*, wearing a Tae Kwando black belt, whose office walls were adorned with posters proclaiming the country as the original home of Voodoo, who married us in his office. The mayor began the ceremony by giving me one last chance to reconsider the action upon which I was about to embark. He proclaimed that from this moment on, my name would be forever stricken from the ranks of the *celibitaires* (bachelors). I nodded that I understood and was happy with my decision. Most black Americans come to Africa to find their heritage, I came and found my destiny, Arese.

After a couple of days of honeymoon in Cotonou, which involved visiting historical sights and museums, we returned to Lagos. The Deputy Chief of Mission (DCM) Tibor Nagy and his wife Jane hosted a reception for us to introduce me to the American embassy personnel. Now that I was the American Ambassador's wife, to avoid a conflict of interest I gave up my medical consultancy and business. I became the honorary president of the American Women's Club (AWC) and a member of the spouses of Heads' of

Missions group. My duties included charities, hosting and attending receptions and dinners.

As an Ambassador's wife, I was encouraged to apply immediately for my United States citizenship and to pledge my allegiance to its flag. Apparently, when a foreigner is married to a diplomat on post, the citizenship process is expedited. I had to fill in all the necessary forms, which were sent to the US citizens and immigration office in Maryland for processing. Without delay a date was set for my interview. To prepare, I got a crash course on American history and politics by reading the *Manual for Citizenship* published by the Daughters of the American Revolution. Walter took some rest and restoration (R&R) time so he could accompany me to Baltimore for my interview.

We arrived in Washington, D.C a couple of days prior and took a train to Baltimore for the interview. When we arrived at the waiting room of the Immigration and Naturalization Services (INS) building, I saw throngs of people waiting anxiously for their interview. As soon as we showed our embassy identifications, passports and my interview form, we were ushered straight in to the room of a senior official. She asked me a couple of questions about American history and politics. The questions were basic and easy. She then said I had passed my test, congratulated me and gave me a flag. She offered us tea and talked to us for a while. Everyone was extremely friendly. To this day, I tell people I had a very good experience with the INS.

We left the building and headed back to the train station. As we walked there I proudly held on to my flag. I was now a citizen of the United States, "God's own country" to Nigerians. At the station, there was a man looking dejected, half asleep on a bench. When he saw me holding my flag, he suddenly sat up and asked, "What day is it and why are you holding a flag?" He must have felt time had passed him by and he had lost count of the days. I smiled back and told him that I had just gotten my U.S citizenship and that was why I was holding my flag. He looked at me and replied sarcastically, "Big deal." He laid straight back on the bench and went to sleep. I felt he was taking his citizenship for granted, the very freedoms and liberty so many people around the world long for. I was now a patriotic American citizen and believed in America's ideals.

Walter had some friends who decided to host a welcoming luncheon party for me. On our way, as we stopped for a red light at an intersection, the car behind us smashed into our car with such force that it propelled us into the vehicle in front of us. I felt a sharp pain in my neck. Luckily, we were wearing our seat belts. The next thing I remember was hearing police and ambulance sirens. Walter kept asking "Honey, are you alright?" I told him I felt a pain in my neck so I would not move my head. The paramedics came to me in the car and asked "Ma'm are you okay?" I replied that my neck hurts. They put a collar round my neck and said "Ma'am, we are taking you to the hospital." I looked at them and said, "Wait, let me ask my husband." They looked at each other in disbelief then looked at me, simultaneously saying "Ma'am, it's your life."

I suddenly realized that I had expressed an internalized cultural submission. The need for permission from one's husband is an idea that patriarchal society puts in women. It had come spontaneously out of me, a successful independent physician. Our environment and culture has a strong impact on us and influences our decision making. At times, that culture may be at odds with logic. I looked at the paramedics and said, "Let's go." Walter asked them what hospital they were taking me to and said he would meet me there. After x-rays and scans, I was relieved to learn I had not fractured any bone. However, I had whiplash. I had to wear a neck brace for the rest of our vacation.

CHAPTER TWENTY FOUR

War of words ... The Battle for democracy

A S SOON AS WE GOT back to Nigeria I was immediately issued an American diplomatic passport. Nigeria was going through a very difficult, dangerous and turbulent time. Again the citizens were defenseless against a brutal dictator, General Sani Abacha. My greatest duty would be joining Walter in defending the Nigerian people. I would assist and stand beside him, giving him the full support he needed as he identified with and stood beside the Nigerian people in their resistance to tyranny. Once more we found ourselves in a conflict involving soldiers; only this time, we were together and it was not a civil war. We were fighting an authoritarian government run by the armed forces. It was a battle fought with words against brutality, a duty to speak out against despotism.

It all started when the hopes of Nigerians that their votes would usher in a new dawn of democratic rule were shattered when General Ibrahim Babaginda, annulled the freest and fairest elections on June 12, 1993. Moshood Abiola was the proclaimed winner of that contest. He was a business tycoon and philanthropist. Although a Yoruba Muslim from the South, he broke through both religious and ethnic barriers in the country. I remember casting my vote for him, the Social Democratic party candidate, popularly referred to by his initials, MKO. I had watched and listened to the returns and rejoiced at the thought of having a democratically elected president, only to have that jubilation truncated by the election's annulment. I felt irate and robbed. Millions of other Nigerians were enraged as well. They took to the streets in protest. The unrest that followed the next few months was more than what General Babaginda had bargained for.

Under pressure from many sides, Babaginda knew he could no longer control the situation and unceremoniously announced that he would step aside. On 26 August 1993, he appointed an interim national government, headed by Yoruba lawyer and industrialist Ernest Shonekan. Babaginda may have thought that by selecting Shonekan, who was a traditional chief from the same town as Chief MKO Abiola, he could pacify most Nigerians. He was wrong. The protests continued. People demanded the elections be honoured. Civil unrest continued and strikes began after the interim national government reduced the fuel subsidy, which caused hikes in fuel prices. Chief Shonekan was head of State for less than three months. On 17 November 1993, General Sani Abacha, Chief of Defense Staff and Minister of Defense, decided to take over under the pretext of restoring order. He executed a bloodless coup on the Shonekan-led interim government.

At the seat of power in Aso Rock, Abuja, General Abacha met with stake holders and promised to release imprisoned MKO and hand power back to democratic civilian rule. He also met with diplomats and had a detailed meeting with Walter. The diplomats were hopeful that he would keep to his word; even some of MKO's followers agreed to be part of his cabinet. When I heard General Abacha had promised to hand over power to democratic civilian rule soon, I was skeptical. I remember telling Walter, "There is no way General Abacha will hand over power to civilian rule. He has been involved in coups that have brought other officers to power, and like a tornado he has been circling the power base craving to rule. This is his opportunity and he will not let it go."

General Abacha did not restore civilian rule. He would prove to be one of the most brutal dictators Nigeria ever had.

After unsuccessfully trying to get the military to declare him the winner of the elections, MKO decided to call a press conference. On 11 June 1994, at Epetedo, Lagos, he declared himself the winner of the elections and thus the rightfully elected president of the Federal Republic of Nigeria. He said he would constitute his cabinet in due time and called his Government a Government of National Unity (GNU). His declaration is referred to as The Epetedo Declaration. In the late night of June 22, 1994, under orders from General Abacha the military arrested Abiola on charges of treason and threw him into jail. MKO's arrest did not go down well with the masses. The atmosphere was volatile. Civil rights groups and international human rights organization were appalled and began to press for his release.

Walter and I had just arrived in Boston on vacation and to watch the FIFA World Cup game between Argentina and Nigeria. We had prime seats for the game, which was scheduled for June 25, 1994. As soon as Abiola was arrested, Walter got a call from the State Department in Washington and the American embassy in Lagos informing him of the developments. He immediately had to cut short his vacation and we returned to Lagos. His sister Marylyn and her friend became the beneficiaries of our precious tickets.

The military dictatorship felt they could go through me to ensure they did not get any opposition from Walter. I was surprised when they sent the wife of a general to pay me a visit and ask me to name anything I wanted to keep Walter quiet. I made it clear that there was nothing I wanted that was more important than standing up for the oppressed people of Nigeria. The general's wife left disappointed, unable to accomplish her mission. To sell one's conscience is inconceivable, and I am glad my parents instilled such values in me. That visit made me realize that the regime was going to use any means to stay in power.

In another encounter at Aso Rock, the seat of power, some generals' wives again tried to persuade me to convince Walter to stop being so outspoken against Abacha. General Abacha's wife, Maryam, summoned all spouses of Heads of Diplomatic Missions to a gathering there. It was meant to be for her to get acquainted with the spouses. I flew into Abuja with some of the other wives of diplomats. We all went to Aso Rock in an official bus that was sent to the hotel to pick us up. Most of the senior army officer's wives were also in attendance. As the wife of the American Ambassador, I was chosen by the other spouses to give the message of thanks on behalf of the diplomatic spouses. After the gathering, I was approached by General Abacha's wife and another general's wife. They said they were saddened that my husband was so harsh on General Abacha in the media and asked whether there was a way I could convince him to soften his stance and tone down his criticisms? They suggested I should use my feminine prowess during intimate times to convince him. Again I was dismayed at their suggestion and approach. I turned to them and said:

> My husband, Walter, loves Nigeria and does not want her to continue to be a pariah nation. It is out of love that he continues to stress that your husband, General Abacha, is going down the wrong path. I am sure he would rather tell him this privately but he has not been able to secure a meeting with the General. Your husband's close aides have been blocking any possibility of a meeting. I think it is important we get both our husbands to meet and discuss concerns. When a mother scolds a child who is going down the wrong path, it is out of love for that child. What my

husband is doing is not personal, it is for the good of
the country and in support of what is right.

Maryam immediately said she would speak to her husband.
She asked if my husband could meet with her husband later that
evening. She promised to call me around 7:30pm. She was gentle
and seemed sincere. She expressed her thanks. I joined the other
spouses on the bus and returned to the hotel. Walter, who had
been in the American Embassy office Abuja for the last few days,
was surprised at the outcome of the encounter. He was, however,
skeptical that Abacha's security officers and close aides would allow
the meeting to take place. They did not want Abacha to change
course. At about 7:30pm, a senior security officer called our hotel
room to inform us that the meeting General Abacha's wife had set
up would not take place. It seemed that, for Abacha, there was no
going back.

The National Democratic Coalition (NADECO) was an
umbrella organization for all the country's pro-democracy and
human rights group. Its members were actively and aggressively
challenging military rule and oppression. Walter and the American
Embassy became a shield for NADECO. Nonetheless, on October
6, 1995 Pa Rewane, an elderly chieftain of the organization, was
assassinated at his house. It was widely believed that the murder
was carried out by the military government.

Abacha felt that some of the resistance he was getting from
activists could be solved if he could get rid of Walter, whom he
described as a thorn in his side. There were three assassination
attempts on Walter's life.

Abacha's government grew desperate to do away with Walter
and embassy security personnel were very concerned for his safety.
They suggested Walter have round-the-clock bodyguards, but
he refused. The State Department had to send for the Nigerian
ambassador to the United States to express its concern over the

matter. I also became very apprehensive for Walter's safety but I continued to encourage and support him. I was always touched by numerous messages I received from the Nigerian people, letting me know they were praying for us, especially about our safety. Walter was not deterred by the threats to his life but actually was embolden by them.

I remember one morning after he had just left for work, a domestic staff ran to tell me "Madam, Ambassador has been hit." I was beside myself, I asked: "Where is he?" The staff replied: "In his car on the street." With all that had been going on, horrific thoughts began to go through my mind. I got on the phone and tried to get his secretary at the embassy, but her line was engaged. I then called one of our security guards to go and find out what was happening. I eventually got through to his secretary in the embassy who informed me that Walter was fine, but the car had been rammed at an intersection and gotten spun around. She said the Regional Security Officer was at the site of the incident and another armored car had been sent for the Ambassador. She said the Ambassador and his driver had obeyed protocol and remained in the armored car till help arrived. It seemed because my radar was on high alert, I had forgotten that when a car 'jams' another car in Nigeria it is locally referred to as 'hit.' It turned out to be an innocent incident, but one could never be too cautious.

Abacha seemed increasingly paranoid. He alleged that there had been a coup attempt and rounded up suspects, both military and civilian. General Obasanjo, who was out of the country, was amongst the accused. Obasanjo phoned Walter, who confirmed the rumour and advised him not to return home. Obasanjo was adamant and did return, only to be arrested by Abacha, who had been a junior officer to him in the army. A special court martial tried the accused coup plotters. They were found guilty and given lengthy jail sentences. Most people believed it was a phantom coup, used to silence both military and civilian opponents threatening

Abacha's brutal rule. Major General Shehu Musa Yar'Adua, a retired Nigerian military officer, a fine gentleman and seasoned politician was also thrown into jail. He would later die there under mysterious circumstances.

Walter was very distraught by the death of Shehu Musa Yar'Adua. He had met him a number of times before he was imprisoned. He told me he found Yar'Adua a brilliant politician who understood the tenets of democracy. After Yar'Adua's death Walter communicated his concern to General Obasanjo in prison through his wife Stella[19].

Walter continued to send cables to State Department in Washington regarding the human right abuses occurring in Nigeria. In 1995, former President Jimmy Carter paid a personal visit to Nigeria to evaluate the situation, meet with General Abacha regarding the human rights situation, and assess the prison conditions under which Obasanjo was being held. His wife Rosalyn Carter accompanied him and the embassy assigned me to host her on the site visits that had been scheduled. Walter and I flew into Abuja to meet them. Stella Obasanjo came to the embassy residence and flew into Abuja with us. She had requested a meeting with President Carter and the embassy obliged. Stella was so dedicated in her effort to get her husband released. In her numerous visits to me at the embassy residence, her commitment and devotion to her husband shone.

The morning we arrived in Abuja, we went straight to the international airport to receive the Carters, who were traveling on a chartered jet. President Carter later met with some pro-democracy and human rights groups. He also had a meeting with Stella Obasanjo. He said he would discuss with General Abacha whether it was possible to improve the conditions under which General Obasanjo was being held. Carter hoped that Obasanjo could be kept under house arrest instead of a prison cell.

---

19 Stella Obasanjo died in 2008

On the morning of the meeting, Mrs. Carter told me she needed to attend the private meeting General Abacha was having with her husband. She said she took her own private notes at meetings and was able to get a sense of the person with whom her husband was meeting. I told her that a schedule had been prepared for her to visit some of the local villages to meet with the women, but I would find out from the embassy personnel if she could sit in on the meeting. She gave me a piece of advice I have never forgotten which has helped me in my marriage. She implied to me that she went almost everywhere her husband went and took an interest in what he was doing, including taking notes for him. This, she said, helps to keep a couple bonded together, instead of them growing apart.

The embassy staff agreed to allow us to attend the meeting briefly, before continuing with the preplanned schedule. President and Mrs. Carter, Walter and I and some embassy staff went to the meeting. The American delegation was introduced and I remember as I was being introduced, General Abacha suddenly said out loud, "She is our sister and does not need introduction." President Carter seemed a bit surprised. Later that night at the official state banquet, I was seated next to President Carter. He asked me if I was really General Abacha's sister, I smiled and told him 'No.' The term 'my sister' or 'my brother' was commonly used in Nigeria but did not mean one was related. It seemed that he gave a sigh of relief. He must have been wondering how the background check could have missed such a basic fact.

When we left Abuja we went to Enugu, where President Carter had established a guinea worm eradication project that had helped transform the lives of so many villagers. When we arrived at one of the villages in Enugu, Carter was given a village title that referred to him as their saviour.

Schedule of Carter's visit to Abuja, Nigeria

<u>Schedule for the</u>
<u>Visit to Abuja of</u>
<u>The Honorable Jimmy Carter and Mrs. Carter</u>
<u>20-22 March 1995</u>

<u>Monday, 20 March 1995</u>

1440	President and Mrs. Carter and travelling party arrive Abuja International Airport, Presidential Terminal. Met by Ministry of Foreign Affairs officials and Ambassador and Mrs. Carrington.
1455	Proceed by motorcade to Nicon Noga Hilton.
1530	Arrive at hotel. Unscheduled time.
1745	Private meeting in President Carter's suite.
1830	Briefing by Ambassador Carrington, assisted by OIC Andrews, PAO Hull, Peace Corps Director Spellman, Economic Counselor Yarvin and Agricultural Attache House - Room 612.
1950	Depart hotel for Sheraton Hotel Ballroom.
2000	Arrive Sheraton for dinner hosted by Secretary to the Government of the Federation Alhaji Aminu Saleh.
2215	Dinner ends; return to Hilton.

<u>Tuesday, 21 March 1995</u>

0930	Depart Hotel for Wuse Market.
0945	Arrive Wuse.
1025	Depart Wuse for Ministry of Foreign Affairs.
1030	Arrive MFA for meeting with Minister of Foreign Affairs (TBN).
1120	Depart MFA for Ministry of Water Resources.
1130	Arrive for meeting with Minister of Water Resources (TBN).
1220	Depart for Ministry of Health Liaison Office.
1230	Arrive for meeting with Minister of Health (TBN).
1320	Depart for hotel.
1330	Arrive hotel. No-host lunch at poolside.
1525	Depart hotel for New Federal Secretariat.
1530	Arrive for meeting with Secretary to the Government Federation Alhaji Aminu Saleh.
1615	Tour of Abuja (With Federal Capital Development Authority).
1715	Tour ends. Proceed to State House.
1730	Meeting with Head of State.
1830	Meeting ends;. return to hotel.
1930	Meeting with National Constitutional Conference delegates in Lagos Room at hotel.
2045	Meeting ends. Unscheduled time.

<u>Wednesday, March 22 1995</u>

0800	Press Conference.
0830	Depart for Airport.
0905	Arrive Airport.
0915	Wheels up for Enugu.

The greatest international cry against the brutal regime of Abacha would result from the execution of Ken Saro Wiwa and the other eight Ogoni activists, commonly referred to as the Ogoni Nine. The Niger delta region, produces oil which provides the national revenue and is home to the Ogoni people. This region had been subjected to untold environmental degradation and undue suffering, morbidity and mortality to its population. Ken Saro Wiwa, a poet, playwright, author and social activist, decided to take up the banner for his people as they cried out against the oil companies, especially Shell, and the Nigerian military government. He led the Movement for the Survival of Ogoni People (MOSOP), and was so effective in his activism that he was able to gain the support and attention of some international environmental groups.

This did not go down well with General Abacha. The Ogoni Nine were arrested and accused of being involved in the killings of some Ogoni elders who had a favorable disposition to the military government. It was widely believed that the trial of the Ogoni Nine in November 1995 was a sham. They were convicted and given the death penalty by the government convened tribunal. This judgment had diplomats, local and international activist scrambling to see if the death penalty could be lifted. Diplomatic cables flew back and forth.

November 10, 1995 was supposed to be a happy event: the annual Marine Corps Ball celebration at the American Embassy. It would be my first Marine Corps Ball as the ambassador's wife and a day to show appreciation for the good work the Marines who guard the embassy do. Walter was swamped by the diplomatic tirade over the Ogoni Nine. He told me he needed to make a quick trip to Abuja to meet with General Abacha to try to convince him not to execute the Ogoni Nine. He left that morning, and while he was in the air they were executed. He landed, only to be told by the embassy staff who met him at the airport that the Ogoni Nine had just been killed. Walter was furious and disheartened. He returned to Lagos and cabled Washington. He met with other ambassadors and heads of missions to discuss the issue. There was an immediate uproar and condemnation from around the world. That same day, the United States and over two dozen countries recalled their ambassadors in protest.

When Walter arrived at the residence he briefed me on what was happening. He dressed in his tuxedo and we left for the Ball. He would use the event to update the American community, embassy staff and the Marines. He gave a brilliant speech on the ideals of the United States of America and its role in upholding the truths in the Declaration of Independence. He also said, in protest against the execution of Ken Saro Wiwa and the other Ogoni activists, that he had been recalled by the State Department. He thanked the Marines for the role they played round the world. That evening was a somber one due to the events of the day. The next morning, Walter was on a flight back to the State department in Washington D.C.

Marine Corps Ball 1995

I would spend the next five months at the Embassy residence holding down the fort and hoping he would return soon. Our first

Christmas as a married couple and wedding anniversary would be spent apart.

When Walter returned to Nigeria around the middle of April 1996, he was even more determined to confront the brutal regime. The people were filled with terror. Abacha had made it clear that he would not tolerate any form of opposition. He had spies who were reporting on activities of the pro-democracy and human rights organizations.

Kudirat, the wife of Chief M.K.O Abiola, the presumed winner of the annulled elections, was shot on the fourth of June 1996 on her way to the Canadian High Commission. She was going there to push for, amongst other requests, sanctions against the Abacha regime. She died from the gunshot wounds to her head. Her driver died also, but her aide Sofolahan, who was said to have been in the car with her survived. He was later accused of being the one that had betrayed her and collaborated with the military to murder her.

The weekend before Kudirat Abiola was gunned down, John Shattuck, the U.S. Assistant Secretary of State for Democracy and Human Rights, was in Nigeria to meet with individuals, pro-democracy and human rights groups to assess the situation. Some of the scheduled meetings were to take place at the Ambassador's Residence. An embassy staff member contacted me with a list of the names and time slots of the different individuals or groups that would be meeting with John Shattuck. To ensure each individual could talk in privacy, the embassy staffer and I set up a system. When individuals or groups arrived, they were seated in separate waiting areas. When it was their turn, they would go into the private room where their meeting with Walter, John Shattuck and the embassy's political counsel took place. After their meeting, they would not be allowed back into the waiting area but had to leave immediately through a different exit. The next person would then be ushered into the meeting room.

So many people and groups had requested to meet with John

Shattuck. A number of wives whose husbands had been thrown in jail were on the schedule. Although Kudirat had a long scheduled meeting with John Shattuck at the Embassy the day before, she came to the Ambassador's residence to meet with him again. The image of Kudirat in the waiting area before her appointment is still vivid in my mind. She seemed so full of life and enthusiasm. She embraced me and talked about her children and the toll their father's imprisonment was having on them. She analyzed their different characters and their coping abilities. She talked about her daughter Hafsat who was a student at Harvard. She felt optimistic about all the international attention her husband's case was getting, including the high profile visit from an undersecretary.

Her meeting lasted longer than scheduled. Shortly after she left, I got a message from the security guards at the gate that she wanted to return. The guards were instructed that once people left they could not come back in unless their names were resubmitted to the gate. Kudirat told the guards to call me because she was coming back to see me, not Walter or Shattuck. I asked the guard to allow her in. She said she had forgotten to mention something very important at the meeting and needed a minute to convey the information. I spoke to the embassy personnel in charge of the meetings and asked if she could be allowed back in for a minute. Although they were not meant to, he obliged me. When she finished she came looking for me to thank me. Walter came out briefly from the meeting and joined me as I was waving goodbye to Kudirat. He teased me and said Kudirat and I pulled a stunt by getting her in a second time. That was the last time we would see Kudirat alive.

Schedule of Shattuck's visit-Individuals and groups he met with. 1 of 2

SCHEDULE FOR A/S SHATTUCK VISIT TO NIGERIA

WEDNESDAY, MAY 29, 1996:

1945 ARRIVE LAGOS ON LUFTHANSA FLIGHT 574. PROCEED TO AMBASSADOR'S RESIDENCE FOR BRIEFING.

THURSDAY, MAY 30, 1996:

0505 GUESTS AT GQ PICKED UP

0525 DEPART AMBASSADOR'S RESIDENCE FOR DOMESTIC AIRPORT

0655 DEPART FOR ABUJA

0755 ARRIVE ABUJA INTERNATIONAL AIRPORT

0830 CHECK IN TO NICON NOGA HILTON HOTEL.

0930 BRIEFING AT USLO

1030 MEETING WITH LEGAL ADVISOR AUWALU YADUDU (CONFIRMED) AT A/S HOTEL ROOM

1200 MEETING WITH FOREIGN MINISTER IKIMI (CONFIRMED) AT MFA

1300 BUFFET LUNCHEON WITH NGO LEADERS AT OIC RESIDENCE

1500 MEETING WITH TRANSITION ADVISOR SULE HAMMA (CONFIRMED) AT NEW FEDERAL SECRETARIAT

1630 MEETING TRANSITION IMPLEMENTATION COMMITTEE CHAIRMAN MAMMAN NASIR (TENTATIVE) AT CONFERENCE CENTER

1800 TBD

2000 DINNER WITH NORTHERN POLITICAL FIGURES AT NICON NOGA HOTEL

FRIDAY, MAY 31, 1996:

0630 BREAKFAST AND CHECKOUT

0720 DEPART FOR AIRPORT

0825 DEPART ABUJA FOR LAGOS

0925 ARRIVE LAGOS DOMESTIC AIRPORT

Schedule of Shattuck's visit-Individuals and groups he met with. 2 of 2

1025 ARRIVE EMBASSY. ARRANGE PER DIEM AND ADMIN DETAILS, BRIEFING BY COUNTRY TEAM.

1200 MEETING WITH KUDIRAT ABIOLA AND CHIEF AWOSIKA (CONFIRMED) AT EMBASSY (10 PEOPLE EXPECTED)

1330 BREAK (CASUAL LUNCH FOR A/S SHATTUCK, CHARLES COHEN, MCARTHUR DE SHAZER, ERICA BARKS-RUGGLES, AND EMBASSY PEOPLE, 8 PEOPLE EXPECTED)

1500 MEETING WITH PRISCILLA KUYE (CONFIRMED) AND CHIEF KUYE AT AMBASSADOR'S RESIDENCE (10 PEOPLE EXPECTED)

1630 MEETING WITH LABOR ACTIVISTS AT AMBASSADOR'S RESIDENCE (17 PEOPLE EXPECTED)

1845 MEETING WITH MRS. FALANA, JITI OGUNYE, REPRESENTATIVE OF GANI FAWEHINMI'S CHAMBERS, AND NCP REPRESENTATIVE (TENTATIVE) AT AMBASSADOR'S RESIDENCE (13 PEOPLE EXPECTED)

2030 DINNER WITH JOURNALISTS AT AMBASSADOR'S RESIDENCE TO DISCUSSION PRESS REPRESSION ON BACKGROUND (INVITATIONS SENT, NO RESPONSES YET) (20 PEOPLE EXPECTED)

SATURDAY, JUNE 1, 1996:

0800 MEETING WITH AYO OBE (TENTATIVE) AND OLISA AGBAKOBA (CONFIRMED) AT AMBASSADOR'S RESIDENCE (12 PEOPLE EXPECTED)

0945 MEETING WITH STELLA OBASANJO AND CHIEF OLAPADE (CONFIRMED) AT AMBASSADOR'S RESIDENCE (10 PEOPLE EXPECTED)

1130 MEETING WITH ABOSEDE RANSOME-KUTI (TENTATIVE) (10 PEOPLE EXECTED)

1300 BREAK (CASUAL LUNCH FOR A/S SHATTUCK'S PARTY AND EMBASSY GROUP, 8 PEOPLE EXPECTED)

1400 MEETING WITH HUMAN RIGHTS ACTIVISTS AT AMBASSADOR'S RESIDENCE (CONFIRMED) (14 PEOPLE EXPECTED)

1600 PRESS CONFERENCE AT AMBASSADOR'S RESIDENCE (GUESTIMATE OF 35 PEOPLE EXPECTED)

1820 DEPART FOR AIRPORT

2020 A/S SHATTUCK DEPARTS FOR GENEVA ON SABENA FLIGHT 522

2145 REST OF PARTY DEPARTS FOR WASHINGTON ON VIA FRANKFURT ON LUFTHANSA FLIGHT 565

As soon as Walter heard of Kudirat's death, he went with some embassy staff to pay condolences to her family. The international community would make her funeral a show of solidarity in opposition to the military. Walter met with several of the other ambassadors and suggested that they should all attend her funeral service. The British High Commissioner and the Canadian High Commissioner were very supportive of the idea. They usually joined Walter in the forefront to register their disapproval of the Abacha's regime abuses. However, some of the other ambassadors felt that, as diplomats, they should look the other way. Even though they were not pleased with what was going on, they felt their primary duty was to observe events and report to their home office. I remember one of the European ambassadors coming to discuss this with me at the residence. He said Walter was rallying all the ambassadors to go to Kudirat's funeral as a show of solidarity and opposition to the brutality happening. He said he wanted to let me know he would not be attending because it could be dangerous, and there might be an outbreak of violent clashes between the people and the military. He said some people are cut out to be martyrs and maybe Walter was, but he did not come to Lagos to be one. He asked me to let Walter know his views. However, a good number of diplomats did attend the funeral, much to the annoyance of the military.

With Chief MKO Abiola in prison, Kudirat's young children were essentially without any parent to care for them and their safety was in question. After their mother's funeral, Walter recommended and helped facilitate their visas to live with relatives in the United States. The nation and indeed the world were again shocked by the viciousness of the Abacha government. Kudirat was a gentle soul, a loving mother and businesswoman whose husband's election victory annulment and subsequent imprisonment threw her into the limelight. She had become a vocal rallying point for the pro-democracy groups. In her attempt to ensure that her husband's mandate was not lost she achieved greatness and her assassination made her a martyr to the cause of democracy.

CHAPTER TWENTY FIVE

The "good-fight"...Build up and final showdown

THAT SAME YEAR, 1996, WALTER's stepmother died. I tried to take as much burden of dealing with the details of her funeral off his shoulders as I could. I knew how important the struggle for Nigerian democracy was, and that it needed his full attention. I contacted the funeral home in San Francisco and made sure all the arrangements were in place. Walter and I attended her funeral and returned directly back to Nigeria. Later, when Walter's only sibling, his sister Marylyn, was diagnosed with breast cancer, it was me she turned to for support because she did not want to burden her brother or have him lose focus on the "good fight" for Nigeria. Although I could not take away the personal emotions he was going through during these periods, I tried to at least pick up the additional strain he would have had dealing directly with these issues. I worried about the effects of the stress on his health, so I did everything possible to absorb some of the burden.

The Embassy Regional Security Officer (RSO), named Mike, used to come round to the Ambassador's residence to check on and brief the security staff. He would also have briefings with me. I began to realize as Ambassador's wife I had to be conscious of security and secrecy. As a result of the hostility from the military dictatorship, it was not safe for me to go to certain areas. I started to feel like a foreigner in my homeland, having to abide by all the warnings to which expatriates are asked to adhere to.

Walter and I sometimes strolled around the garden at the residence. One evening, as we walked, he told me he was about to embark on a direct confrontation with the military dictatorship in defense and support of the Nigerian peoples' human rights and a return to democracy. He felt he had a duty beyond merely being a diplomat who observed and reported back to his home country. He had to speak out in a time of tyranny. It would be a mission fraught with risk that would expose my family and me to peril, so he wanted my views.

I told him I fully supported him and no matter how dangerous it was, I would stand beside him all the way. I told him that I wanted generations to come to judge us favorably, so it was important that we stood for justice against injustice, humanity against inhumanity, kindness against brutality, love against hatred and courage against cowardice. I felt it was important that we contribute to the betterment of mankind. I understood the need for us to stand by Nigerians during this time of oppression. For Nigeria to have a stable democracy, it needed to focus not just on the technical aspect of elections but on the entire electoral process, institution building, strengthening of opposition parties and civil society. Those elected needed to be transparent and held accountable. It was an opportunity and privilege for me to help reinstate democracy in Nigeria even if it was fraught with risk. I told Walter I believed strongly in our marriage and unity. I summed up my belief about marriage thus:

> Marriage is about a union, joining together of two, a
> combination locked together,
> A separated marriage beats that objective.
> A marriage should be united in all fronts and united
> against all confrontation

A marriage cannot be divided,
A divided marriage is an oxymoron.

The dangers were omnipresent. Much later, Walter and I faced paramilitary troops at gunpoint during a private farewell party being held for us. As Walter battled the military regime, I became directly involved in the struggle for human rights and democracy in Nigeria. Pro-democracy groups, activist and individuals began to consult with me and I became a conduit for their messages to Walter. I read through and gave an input on almost every speech Walter gave.

In acknowledging the role I played in assisting Walter in the pro-democracy fight Nobel laurate Wole Soyinka in the book "A friend in Need: Tributes to Ambassador Walter Carrington @80" stated:

> "Let me use this occasion to pay public tribute also to someone not so prominently recognised in this undertaking: Walter was constantly aided by no less than Arese, the wife that he took from this land, as if to cement his commitment to its people in a way that went beyond politics and translated as no less than a blood bond between us, right here, and that other 'us' that had survived the horrors of the transatlantic slave passage."

There were political prisoners in jail and presses were shut down and journalists were hunted, killed, or imprisoned for writing the truth about the military rulers. Nigeria was in the international news; its leaders had made it a pariah nation. For the Western world, the view of Nigeria had gone from great expectations to great exasperation.

In January 1997, Walter and I returned to the U.S. briefly to attend President Clinton's second inauguration. He also attended some meetings at the State Department. Nigeria was a great source of concern to the United States. Even though there were gross human rights abuses and a military dictatorship in power, the nation still relied heavily on Nigeria for its supply of oil. Since 1993, Walter had continually been pressing for greater sanctions on Nigeria's dictatorship government, but many chief executive officers of American businesses in Nigeria felt more sanctions would hurt their economic opportunities in the country.

The normal tour of duty for an Ambassador is three years. Walter had already spent four years and was now preparing our return to America because his tour was ending. Several people who were brave enough to show their appreciation and disapproval of the brutal military regime organized farewell parties for us. Abacha was out to deal with anyone associating with Walter. Some people who wanted to remain beneficiaries of the corrupt government and others who were scared of being assassinated kept their distance. Amongst the determined, however, were people like Chief T.O.S Benson, brother of Bobby Benson, the highlife guru of the sixties. He and his wife hosted a splendid party for us. Retired General Theophilus Danjuma, who played a major role in the Nigerian civil war, and his wife also gave us a farewell party.

Chief Omowale Kuye and his wife Priscilla, an activist and former head of the Nigerian Bar Association (NBA) gave us a rousing farewell party. They presented us with specially woven traditional outfits called 'Aso Oke' which we changed into at the venue.

Chief Lawrence Fabunmi, a former Nigerian ambassador to Turkey, Zambia and Poland who was a friend of my parents hosted a particularly memorable farewell party for us. My father had suffered a stroke and was in hospital in London, my mother by his side. Fabunmi's party touched my heart because I saw him as filling in for my parents. It rained heavily on the day of the party, but people still attended and did not mind getting drenched under the sun canopies outdoors. The day was almost marred when Chief

Fabunmi nearly got electrocuted while holding the microphone. The rain eventually subsided and the party went on with various groups delivering solidarity speeches.

At each party during our farewell tour, Walter would use the opportunity to give very direct speeches attacking the brutality of the military regime and citing the importance of human rights. He roused the crowds by charging them to continue to demand democracy. The press soaked in everything and gave his speeches headline attention. Mingled in with the gathered admirers and well-wishers were spies who reported back to Abacha about how, after each party, the people seemed even more encouraged and determined by Walters's speeches. They also reported the list of attendees. Abacha decided that all further farewell parties for Walter should be prevented.

We became aware of this on September 18, 1997, when the pro-democracy and human rights group under the umbrella organization NADECO held a farewell party for Walter and me. They wanted to show their appreciation for our support. The military felt that allowing this party to take place would allow Walter to make a most defiant speech to a most receptive audience. We arrived at the location of the party at the house of the pro-democracy leader Chief Onasanya, in a dense suburb of Lagos called Surulere. As we arrived, we noticed crowds of people lining the streets cheering and waving to us. There were also several military trucks and soldiers in full combat gear. The street leading to chief's home was cordoned off. Our diplomatic car was stopped and a stern looking officer told us that nobody was allowed to go any further. The officer said they had gotten a report of ammunition being delivered to the neighbourhood. We informed them that a farewell party for the American Ambassador was meant to take place at an address on that street. He said he felt it was not safe and apologized that the party could not take place there.

A pro-democracy activist, came to meet us as the officer was talking to us. She told us that the venue had been changed. She got into our car and explained that NADECO suspected the military might try to stop the party; a secret alternate location had been prepared. The officer must have heard what she said because as she led us there, we noticed our diplomatic car was being trailed. With her expertise in using the back roads and with the embassy driver doing some evasive maneuvers, we lost the car trailing us.

We arrived at the alternate venue, Chief Abraham Adesanya's house. It was in a large compound with huge locked metal gates. When the gatekeeper saw the diplomatic license plates he quickly let us in, and then relocked the gates. Diplomats from several other countries and the media had already arrived. When we appeared, people cheered and the party started. The host made a welcome speech and was about to give Walter the microphone to make some remarks. Then we heard large bangs and thumps. There was a lot of commotion going on outside the gates. We heard a military commander asking the soldiers to break down the gates. Everybody stood still and looked towards the gates. Suddenly, the huge gates fell to the ground, revealing several "Operation Sweep" paramilitary Land Rovers. Soldiers in battle gear surrounded the compound with cocked guns pointed at the guests, including the diplomats. Never had I seen so many guns being pointed at unarmed civilians. I had seen Sylvester Stallone surrounded by paramilitary troops in the movie "First Blood," but I had never imagined or expected to be surrounded by armed paramilitary troops at a civilian party that included diplomats protected by international law.

Their commander ran into the venue, panting. As soon as he spotted Walter he said into his radio excitedly, "Sir, sir, we have found them. I can confirm Ambassador Carrington is here. We are about to abort the party." He turned off the radio and ordered everyone to leave the venue. A courageous human rights lawyer, Gani Fawehinmi, took the microphone and said the party would continue because it was a private residence and the military had no

right to forcefully enter and break up the party. A fierce-looking
soldier pointed his weapon directly at Gani and threatened to shoot
him if he did not put down the microphone. Gani tore open his
shirt to expose his broad chest and said to the soldier "Shoot, shoot,
shoot me."

The soldier was about to shoot when his commander realized
that events were in the full view of foreign diplomats and the press.
If bullets started flying, they might cause unintended casualties. He
immediately told the soldier to stand down. He asked Gani not to
endanger the lives of the guests and stated it was better if they all left
peacefully. He told the attendees that he had an order from the very
top to ensure the party did not take place. In response, judging the
gravity of the situation, the host asked the assembled diplomats to
please leave for their own safety. The commander seized all cameras
from the press. Walter and I eventually left, walking side by side.
Everyone remained calm. I fully realized the everyday dangers the
pro-democracy and human rights activist must be going through.

The world's press and foreign services were shocked by such a
brazen attack by the Nigerian military on diplomats from so many
nations, especially the American ambassador. Embassy phones were
ringing off the hook, including ours at the residence. That was the
lead story for some of the American media. *The Washington Post*,
The New York Times and other major newspapers carried the story
as front page news. On September 26, 1997, Howard French wrote
in the *New York Times*,

> Nothing could have prepared Mr. Carrington for
> the seeming final act in his ambassadorship, when
> [Nigerian] state security officials undertook a campaign
> of intimidation against people who have organized
> farewell parties for him. In what Mr. Carrington, a
> 67-year-old lawyer with a 38-year-long familiarity
> with Nigeria called 'the most surrealistic experience

I have had here yet,' heavily armed policemen burst into a well-attended reception in Mr. Carrington's honor in Lagos last week, threatened to shoot one speaker and ordered the foreign guests, including the American Ambassador, to leave at once."

The State Department issued a strong protest to the Nigerian embassy in Washington D.C and demanded an explanation and apology. Because of the actions of the Nigerian military, a farewell party that would probably only have roused the local people became evidence to the world of its brutality and human rights abuses.

NADECO would get a chance to hear Walter's speech at the farewell party the American Embassy itself hosted on October 1997, a few days before we left. Our belongings had already been shipped. We continued to get farewell cards and letters from Nigerians and others thanking us for our support and commitment to restoring democracy. In a card we got from an American Jesuit, Father John Sheehan, he suggested that Walter read the Declaration of Independence for his farewell remarks. Another American, Mark Hansen, who was the CEO of AIICO, an American Insurance company, sent a plaque with a quote from Abraham Lincoln.

As Walter read the Declaration, it seemed significant to what was going on in Nigeria. The press compared the tyranny referred to in the Declaration with that of the Abacha military regime. The power of the Declaration and its connotation was so deep that NADECO felt energized to continue the struggle. Walter said farewell just before the end of the party and read the words of Abraham Lincoln on the plaque given to him: "I do the best I know how, the very best I can, and I mean to keep on doing it to the end. If the end brings me out all right, what is said against me will not amount to anything. If the end brings me out all wrong, ten angels swearing I was right would make no difference."

CHAPTER TWENTY SIX

The Diaspora's struggle

I ONCE TEASED WALTER BY ASKING why he left me behind when I was stranded in Benin and he was the Peace Corps director for Africa who evacuated the American volunteers there. He replied: "It may have taken me a while, but I came back for you." Little did I know that when he came back it would mean that he would 'carry' me to his home country.

America seemed so far away. I never thought I would end up there, yet my unforeseen fate led me there. My husband and I returned to the United States after his tour of duty ended in October 1997. The night we left Lagos, Nigeria, a large crowed of Nigerians including members of NADECO came to the departure terminal at the airport to bid us farewell. Walter who had been given a Nigerian name "Omowale" (which means the child who has returned) by Obasanjo said he hoped to return to Nigeria again under a democratic government.

En route to America, Walter and I stopped over in London to visit my father. He had suffered a stroke in February of that year and was hospitalized in London. I would spend the next couple of weeks by his bedside. I had been in the heat of the struggle for democracy in Nigeria and now I just wanted to be with my father. It was as if he was waiting for me. He died on October 30, 1997.

The evening before he died, I was with him holding his hands. Although he could not talk, he looked at me and smiled. He seemed at peace. Early the next morning, one of my sisters called me to say he had just passed away. I rushed to the hospital; he was still in his room. I held his lifeless hand and cried, talked to him, and then knelt beside his bed and prayed. Walter had already gone ahead to America. I felt so alone in London that day. When we finally left Nigeria, I thought I could breathe a sigh of relief. Instead, I was now filled with grief.

I returned to America to be with Walter, but made arrangements to go back to Nigeria for my father's funeral. After securing a Nigerian visa with much difficulty, I had to fly to London and escort his body back to Nigeria for his funeral. I was advised to only attend the funeral and leave the country immediately since the military dictator was still in power. My safety could not be guaranteed. Going back to a country where I had already faced soldiers at gunpoint was riddled with risk, especially since I no longer had diplomatic immunity. Nevertheless, I had to attend my father's funeral. The notion of not paying him my last respect was one I could not bear. Walter could not go back with me because the State Department felt it was unsafe for him in particular, and the Nigerian embassy probably would not grant him a visa if he applied.

In Nigeria, the U.S. embassy was very supportive. Several members of staff travelled to Benin City for the funeral. I was whisked in to attend the funeral and whisked out again. I could not spend time grieving with my mother and siblings who had come from different parts of the world to mourn. I comforted myself with the thought that I would be able to do that in my husband's arms when I got back home.

Nigerians in Diaspora continued to hope and advocate for a return to democracy in Nigeria. When Walter arrived in America, they saw him as a champion for the cause so our struggle against the brutal military regime continued. As a result, I still could not focus on mourning my father, who had meant so much to me. It was not until eight months later, on Father's day, I broke down and fully grieved for him.

After our arrival, there still seemed to be so much to do for Nigerian democracy in America, sensitizing the American people and the government to what was happening in my homeland. Walter decided to sell the house his mother left to his sister and him, so he could use his part of the funds for the cause. I accompanied him from the East Coast to the West Coast as he spoke at town hall meetings, with members of Congress and different activist groups about the Nigerian situation.

There were many people who felt the U.S. government should be doing more against the Nigerian dictatorship. Walter testified before state legislatures asking them to take the same kind of economic sanctions against Nigeria as they had against apartheid South Africa. He testified before the New York City Council to rename the corner in front of the Nigerian mission to the United Nations as Kudirat Abiola corner to honour the slain wife of the presumed winner of the annulled elections. He stressed that it was his belief that she was assassinated by the Nigerian military dictatorship because she was a leader and a uniting force for the pro-democracy groups.

The day the corner was renamed Kudirat Abiola corner, there was a heavy rain downpour but that did not stop Nigerians in the Diaspora and pro-democracy activists from coming out in large numbers. Chief Anthony Enahoro, Wole Soyinka, Walter and others took turns delivering speeches. Kudirat's eldest daughter Hafsat was there and spoke in honour and remembrance of her mother. It was a victory against the military regime, which had fought hard to prevent the renaming of the corner.

It came to pass that in the same month of June, approximately two years after his dictatorial regime murdered Kudirat Abiola and five years after the annulled elections, Abacha too would meet his demise on June 8, 1998. My husband and I were in Boston when we got a phone call from a newspaper reporter in St. Petersburg, Russia, asking if we could confirm that Abacha had died from an overdose of Viagra. Although the question seemed odd then, later rumours on how he died made that question seem plausible. Nigeria was rampant with celebration over the news of his death. Bars and restaurants were giving out free drinks. There was dancing on the streets and a sense of freedom amongst the people.

Various rumours and theories as to how Abacha died were being spread around. He was said to have a weakness for prostitutes. According to rumours he died after an orgy in the hands of two prostitutes that had been flown in. Another rumour alleged that he died after they fed him a poisoned apple. The official version of his death released by the military was of natural causes. If Abacha had not died, all indications clearly pointed to the fact that he wanted to self-succeed by removing his military uniform and remaining in power as a civilian leader.

Nigeria's June Saga

June 12th 1993- Nigeria's free and fairest elections, presumed winner M.K.O Abiola

June 23rd 1993- Nigeria's elections annulled by General Ibrahim Babangida

June 11th 1994-M.K.O Abiola claims his presidential mandate at Epetedo, Lagos

June 22nd 1994- M.K.O Abiola arrested and imprisoned for treason by Abacha

June 4th 1996 - Kudirat Abiola assassinated by the Abacha military dictatorship

June 8th 1998 - Abacha dies in a 'compromising manner'

General Abdulsalami Abubakar succeeded Abacha. He promised to return Nigeria to democratic rule within a year. He also set free most of the people Abacha had put in prison, including General Obasanjo. He, however, did not free M.K.O Abiola, who needed medical attention. This was an unfortunate mistake because Abiola died in prison under Abubakar's watch. On July 7, 1998, the day he collapsed and subsequently died Abiola was being visited in prison by a United States delegation that included Susan Rice, the Undersecretary of State for African Affairs and Thomas Pickering, a former U.S. ambassador to Nigeria. The death of Abiola has remained a sore point on Abubakar's legacy.

General Abubakar did conduct elections and Obasanjo ran for President and won. On May 29, 1999 Abubakar handed over government to Obasanjo.

Walter and I were invited as special guests to attend the inauguration of the Governor of Lagos state, Bola Ahmed Tinubu and the presidential inauguration of Olusegun Obasanjo. During the celebrations to mark the Lagos state inauguration ceremonies, the governor announced that the street in Lagos where the American Embassy and several other embassies were would be renamed Walter Carrington Crescent. It would be a symbol of appreciation for the role my husband played in promoting the return of democracy to Nigeria and his support for human rights.

CHAPTER TWENTY SEVEN

Defend the defenseless…A father's lasting legacy

WITH NIGERIA NOW BACK TO a democratically elected government, I had time to figure out what I wanted to pursue. I chose to study international public health at Harvard School of Public Health (HSPH). Although my father had died a couple of years previously I still felt the sting of his death. I never forgot the duty he had charged me with: "You must defend the defenseless." It was as if those words continued to guide decisions I made: as a child speaking out and watching out for the less fortunate or those being bullied; from supporting and participating in the struggle for Nigeria's democracy; defending human rights in Nigeria; to studying medicine and finally public health.

At the end of my public health course, I was elected one of the class marshals for life. I also entered the competition to be the graduate speaker for the Harvard commencement of 2000. Cynthia Rossano has written:

Harvard's Commencement is one of very few where students still play so prominent a role. Three students selected in a University-wide competition deliver the parts: first a College senior declaims a Latin salutatory, or address of greeting; then a second senior and a graduate student each deliver an English address. Students choose their own topics. President Josiah Quincy's daughter, describing the 1829 Commencement in her journal, noted that Oliver Wendell Holmes gave a 'funny speech.' In 1853, future president Charles William Eliot spoke on 'The Last Days of Copernicus,' the 'priest who married science to religion.' Phillips Brooks, A.B. 1855, stated, 'It is then a noble thing for a man to have something noble to believe. It gives him strength.' In 1880 Theodore Roosevelt spoke on the 'Practicality of Equalizing Men and Women before the Law.' W.E.B. Du Bois, A.B. 1890, discussed 'Jefferson Davis as a Representative of Civilization,' pointing out that 'As the crowning absurdity, he was the peculiar champion of a people fighting to be free in order that another people should not be free.'

It was a vigorous, month-long competition with entrants from the university's different graduate schools. I was finally selected to give the oration before an audience of tens of thousands of graduates and their families. Even though I was now an American citizen, I was the first Nigerian to ever have this honor. I felt humbled, yet proud. Two of my sisters, one of whom was the sister I had been given the duty to defend, came to my graduation and listened to me give the speech.

I wrote a speech about my experience during the civil war, the duty my father had charged me with, the impact it had had on my life, my choice of profession and the importance of social justice. I titled it "Defend the Defenseless." Both my sisters had tears in their eyes as I talked about the war. We had never really spoken about our experience during that traumatic period. After the speech, they came and hugged me. It was a joyous occasion, but we all had tears in our eyes as we hugged. I guess the memories of the war were flooding through us. We missed our father so much. The memory of his charge lingered on: "You must defend the defenseless."

Two of my nieces were also present. They did not understand the bond we siblings shared or why we had tears in our eyes. They looked at each other and walked towards us and joined in the group hug. I looked up to the sky and for a brief second I believe I saw a rainbow. I smiled; I felt my father's presence. He, too, had joined the group hug. It was as if he were telling us it was all right and now we could at last speak of it. I could relate to the world what it was like to be "a child caught in a war."

PART THREE

ANALYZING LEGENDS, LEGIONS, COUNTRIES AND REGIONS.

POSTSCRIPT

The players... Then and now

I N EVERY WAR THERE ARE legions and there are legends. The legions are usually remembered only in mass except by their families and loved ones. Those few who become legends are the ones who are still widely remembered long after the fighting is done. The list of legends, legions, countries and regions is by no means exhausted in this book. These are some of the players.

Military Players- Officers

For an impressionable child who lived through so cruel a conflict as the Nigerian Civil War, names first heard then continue to hold a special curiosity. The Black Scorpion, Colonel Benjamin Adekunle, leader of the Third Marine Commando Division (3MCD), attained the mythic proportions of a super hero. Only later did I know how he was dreaded by children my age in Biafra, just as the larger than life leader of the secessionist forces, General Chukwuemeka Odumegwu Ojukwu, was by those in the rest of the country.

After thirteen years of exile in Ivory Coast (Côte d'Ivoire) following the end of the Civil War, Ojukwu returned to Nigeria and received a hero's welcome from his fellow Igbo. The people of Nnewi, in Anambra State gave him the chieftaincy title of "Ikemba" meaning power of the people. He was pardoned by the

Nigerian Government in 1983 under President Shehu Shagari. He became active in political life and said, "The surest way to show that the civil war had ended and the Igbo fully integrated into the affairs of the nation was to allow an Igbo to become president." He never did become Nigeria's President but he was clearly the leader of the Igbo. He was revered as the father figure of his fellow Igbo who referred to him till his death in 2011 as "Dikedioramma," the beloved hero. Ironically Ojukwu was born on November 4, 1933 in a town called Zungeru in the Middle Belt of Northern Nigeria, the region of Nigeria he fought so hard to secede from. It is also a quirk of fate that he would spend his dying moments in a hospital in Britain, the same country that he felt had so let him down during the Biafran war.

Despite his military achievements, Adekunle received no such accolades when he was relieved of his command during the war. When he died on 13, December 2014 some people felt he was not given the military honour he deserved for his achievements during the Biafran war. It was his replacement as Commander of the elite unit, General Obasanjo, to whom the Biafrans surrendered, thus ending the terrible conflict. As noted earlier, Obasanjo went on to become both a military and civilian head of state.

General Yakubu Gowon, the ruler of the Federal Republic during the war, was overthrown in a military coup that resulted in General Murtala Muhammed becoming Head of State and Obasanjo becoming Chief of Staff, Supreme Headquarters. Muhammed was later assassinated in a botched coup attempt by Colonel Buka Suka Dimka in February 1976. It was alleged that Colonel Dimka was connected to General Gowon and was trying to restore him to power. General Gowon, who was in exile in England, denied any involvement in the Dimka coup but was still dismissed from the Nigerian army. He was later pardoned of any charges connected to the Dimka coup and reinstated. He returned to Nigeria and took on a role as a respected elder statesman. He focused his attention on altruistic endeavours through his non-profit organization, The Yakubu Gowon Foundation. In an acceptance speech he gave at an event in Lagos in 2012, where he was honored with a Lifetime Achievement Award, Gowon offered sober reflections on the war. He regretted the carnage that resulted from the war. He said, "Whatever the cause, there was no need to go into a civil war." He later implied he was left with no option but to fight in order to keep Nigeria one.

The two great protagonists of the Civil War have in a sense cheated historians. Ojukwu died having never published his detailed account of the war. Gowon still lives, but he too has yet to author a comprehensive memoir of that momentous chapter in the Nation's history.

Major Chukwuma Patrick Nzeogwu was born and spent his early childhood in Kaduna, Nigeria and was nicknamed Kaduna. He spoke English, Hausa and his native Igbo fluently. Whether we are on the side of those who believe he was altruistic or those who believe he was a tribalist, there is no denying that his actions in initiating the first coup in 1966 caused the domino effect that led Nigeria to a civil war and forever changed its history. Did the coup cause the war, or simply accelerate events that were inevitable?

General Obasanjo's view of Nzeogwu is, "Chukwuma had a dream of a great Nigeria that is a force to reckon with in the world, not through ineffective political rhetoric but through purposeful and effective action. He had a dream of an ordered and orderly nation, through a disciplined society. He also dreamt of a country where national interest overrides self, sectional or tribal interest. He wanted a country where a person's ability, output, merit and productivity would determine his social and economic progress, rather than, political, and ethnic considerations."

Brigadier Samuel Ademulegun, a Yoruba, the third highest-ranking military officer, commander of 1st brigade based in Kaduna was a victim of the first coup.

General Aguyi Ironsi, an Igbo officer, put down the first coup. He was the first military ruler and was assassinated during the July retaliatory coup. He remains a legend.

Major Victor Banjo although a Yoruba joined General Ojukwu and fought with the Biafran army. However he was later court-martialed and killed by General Ojukwu. These three military officers, Major Nzeogwu, Major Banjo and General Ironsi never lived to see what became of Nigeria after the civil war but they played a major role in shaping the events leading up to it.

Political Players- Civilians

Chief Obafemi Awolowo was a Founding Father and political leader of the Western region. He was a great thinker, intelligent politician and a planner with great foresight. He was imprisoned on what some felt were trumped-up charges of treasonable felony in 1963. After the war, he was put in charge of the reconstruction. He reentered politics and had a firm grip on the southwest states, but was disliked by some of the eastern states because of his role supporting the Federal government, and by those who felt he was tribalistic. His unsuccessful attempts to become a civilian President of Nigeria has resulted in some people referring to him as "the best President Nigeria never had." His ideas and philosophy are still talked about today and are known as Awoism. He died in 1987.

Chief Nnamdi Azikiwe, a Founding Father from the East and the post-independence Head of State, was born in the Northern town of Zungeru. He was out of the country during the Nzeogwu coup that deposed him. Initially supporting Biafra during the war, he later had a change of heart and supported a united Nigeria. He felt the war was futile and so many Biafrans had lost their lives. Having been a dominant Nigerian Nationalist leader who fought for independence, he also felt Nigeria was stronger as one nation. After the war, he ventured into politics running for President in 1979 without much success. He, however, remained a respected political and father figure in the country till his death at the age of 91 in 1996.

Chief Anthony Enahoro, also a founder, was imprisoned during the pre-coup political turmoil. He was a political leader in the Midwestern region and after the war was very active in politics as a progressive. A brave and outspoken leader against military dictatorship, he had to go into exile during the brutal autocratic years of General Sani Abacha. He would later return to Nigeria as a progressive political force and elder statesman after the death of General Abacha in 1998. As one of the remaining founding fathers, his death in 2010 was seen as the last vestige of an era of altruistic Nigerians who fought for her independence.

Wole Soyinka is a distinguished intellectual and playwright. He is a social critic and fighter for justice, equity, accountability and transparency. He had tried to preempt the impending Biafran war through peaceful settlement. To this end he travelled the length and breadth of Nigeria, including the East, where he met with Brigadier Victor Banjo and General Ojukwu to see how a compromise could be reached. Soyinka was accused of treason and thrown into solitary confinement in a prison cell in the North where he remained for the duration of the war. He would go on to write his famous memoir of that experience in his book titled *"The Man Died: Prison Notes (1972)."* He became the first African to win the Nobel Prize for Literature.

Sardauna of Sokoto, Sir Ahmadu Bello and Prime Minister Tafawa Balewa were casualties of the first coup. As prominent figures in the North, it was the avenging of their deaths that brought about the second coup, which subsequently led to the civil war. They are some of the Legends who paid the ultimate price.

Humanitarian Aid Organizations:

Red Cross, Caritas International, Joint Church Aid, Holy Ghost Fathers of Ireland, and U.S. Catholic Relief Services are among those who helped in alleviating the suffering and fatalities of the

Biafrans during the civil war. The organization Doctors Without Borders (Medecins Sans Frontieres) was formed as a result of the humanitarian crisis some medical volunteers witnessed during the Biafran war. The volunteer medical personnel who serve the organization believe that no one should be denied medical attention because of war. They provide care and relief wherever needed and are not bound by politics, religion or geographical location. The founder, Dr. Bernard Kouchner, later went on to hold several ministerial positions in France, including Minister of Health and Minister of Foreign and European affairs. The organization would later go on to win the Nobel Peace prize.

International Players- The Main Countries and Regions

The truth is "economics trumps at the end of the day." The role played by the United States, Britain, France and the USSR (Russia), more than whatever other reasons they proclaimed, involved some form of economic calculation on their part. Nigeria continued trading with some of these countries throughout the war, exporting commodities like cocoa and ground nut, while some of these international countries continued to invest in Nigeria's oil industry. Their respective national and economic interests assured that none of them officially recognised Biafra. After the war, and till this day, all these countries continue to do billions of dollars worth of business with Nigeria. Today, Nigeria is a major supplier of crude oil to the United States.

Britain

Britain created the amalgamation called Nigeria. It was meant to be a unified country. A divided Nigeria meant failure in their amalgamation. Britain had many millions of pounds of economic interest in Nigeria, so it was in its economic interest that the federal troops of Nigeria succeed. A partly owned British company, Shell-BP Petroleum Development Company, was the first to begin oil exploration in Nigeria and had finally struck commercially viable quantities of crude oil just a few years prior to independence. By the time the civil war started, almost half of Britain's crude oil supply was from Nigeria. In a paper titled "Oil, the British and the Nigerian Civil War," Chibuike Uche stated: "Britain was interested in protecting the investments of Shell-BP in Nigerian oil. In a background note prepared for the Prime Minister on the Nigerian civil war, it was explicitly stated that:

> *To refer publicly in the House to our economic stake in Nigeria would be inadvisable as it would be misunderstood or misrepresented ... Nevertheless, the facts are that Shell and BP have invested at least £250 million in Nigeria on which we now expect a large and increasing return of great importance to the British balance of payments. Other investments are worth up to £175 million. Our annual export trade is about £90 million. 16,000 British subjects live in Nigeria. All this would be at risk if we abandoned our policy of support for the Federal Government and others would be quick to take our place."*

Shell-BP would find itself in a controversial position between Biafra and Nigeria in regard to paying royalties. Although most of Shell's activities were in the Eastern (Biafra) and Midwestern regions, a Nigerian naval blockade of the nation's seaports coerced Shell-BP into paying the royalties to her. Years after the civil war, the Nigerian Government expelled British Petroleum (BP) for supplying fuel to apartheid South Africa. BP's assets were nationalized. Shell, although still heavily involved in Oil exploration and production in Nigeria, continues to be very controversial due to its perceived role in what lead to the killing of the activist Ken Saro Wiwa by the

Abacha regime and the pollution and degradation its oil spills have caused in the Niger Delta region.

Because of its interests, Britain needed to play it safe and bank on the side likely to win the civil war, so it supplied the federal government with a lot of its weaponry. Britain felt that with the size, weaponry, armor and might of the Nigerian army, it should be able to quash the rebellion quickly. However the war continued longer than anticipated.

The British public reacted with shock to the Biafran public relation campaign depicting the humanitarian toll the war was taking. Pictures of starving Biafran children dying from Kwashiorkor (a protein deficient malnutrition) were horrifying and the British public began to put pressure on the prime minister to intervene. With elections coming up in England, Prime Minister Harold Wilson visited Nigeria hoping he could facilitate an end to the war. He also wanted to express the humanitarian concerns of his people. In the last year of the war Britain increased its supply of weapons to Nigeria, but it later got involved in the humanitarian efforts in Biafra.

Five decades after the civil war, Britain's influence on its former colony is much less. Britain still has a lot of economic interest in Nigeria in terms of investments, trade and aid, but China and the U.S. have also moved in. Britain is no longer the main destination of choice for vacation or immigration for Nigerians.

United States

The United States' position on the civil war can be divided into two categories: the official stand of the Johnson and Nixon administrations, and the feelings of the general population. The United States government felt since Nigeria was a British colony, they should take their official stand from that of the British. Like the British, the U.S. did not recognise the State of Biafra and sided with the reunification of Nigeria. Unlike the British however, the U.S. was not supplying weapons to Nigeria.

Regarding public opinion, the campaigns mounted by Biafran public relations consultants were highly effective. Pictures of dying or starving children were brought into people's homes through the television, magazines and newspapers. Foreign journalists in the Biafran territory such as Frederick Forsyth were sending pictures of these children back to the West. No matter who was right or wrong, the toll and suffering of innocent children could not be ignored. The Biafran humanitarian crisis struck a chord with society in the U.S. spawning grassroot humanitarian relief efforts.

American interest in the relief efforts were also demonstrated by actions of some high school students. For example, in November/ December 1968 as young students at Scarsdale High School (SHS) New York (NY), Richard Golob, who is now on the board of United Nations Association of Greater Boston (UNAGB) and Jim Bloom, who is in the Hollywood film industry, spearheaded the Scarsdale Biafra relief campaign, which quickly expanded to include other school districts. The students organized house-to-house campaigns, which over 250 students participated in, collecting money and handing out leaflets. In solidarity with the starving children of Biafra, they conducted a lunch fast at the high school on November 6 and 7, 1968. They went without lunch and watched a film on the Biafran situation in the high school auditorium. They donated their lunch money to the Biafran drive. The funds raised were donated to the Biafra Relief Services Foundation in New York City. Their local newspaper publicized these student campaigns with articles like "Biafran Campaign shows benefits of Student Power." The students were determined to spread the movement as further noted by the article. "At a meeting of Westchester students' councils in Scarsdale this afternoon, Jim will show two movies about the Ibos and try to make the campaign [Westchester, NY] countywide. SHS participants treated the Biafran crisis seriously not as another fad.

They showed in the campaign that SHS student activist do not lack organization, productivity and conviction."

Religious groups and humanitarian bodies began to have fundraisers for Biafran humanitarian relief. As an individual, President-elect Richard Nixon's wife Patricia attended a fundraiser for Biafrans at St Patrick's Cathedral in New York in January, 1969 (Stremlau 1977 pg. 289). Senator Ted Kennedy, a liberal Democrat from Massachusetts, and Senator Strom Thurmond, a conservative republican from South Carolina, pushed for a changed in the U.S. policy and for humanitarian efforts to be increased.

In February 1969, the State Department finally sent a fact finding team to Biafra. The team was led by Senator Charles E. Goodell (R-N/Y) and included Charles W. Dunn for the diplomatic aspects and four experts on Africa led by Jean Mayer, Professor of Nutrition at Harvard School of Public Health. Its findings were scathing. It also talked about overcrowding of hospitals, severe food shortages and disease.

> *"Severe malnutrition underlies all other Biafrian diseases. Severe anemia is widespread among children and pregnant women. Infectious diseases, including measles especially, hit hardest at the very young and the elderly. Tuberculosis, malaria, and dysentery also are prevalent."*

The mission expressed alarm at the low U.S. involvement in the Biafra situation and came up with recommendations the U.S government should take immediately.

The Biafrian Mission Recommends:

1. The fundamental action needed to alleviate suffering in the Nigerian civil war is an immediate ceasefire, for this is the only way that food and medical relief can be adequately provided.

2. The atrocities being inflicted upon Biafrian civilians must be halted.

3. The Biafrans need a greatly expanded tonnage of relief supplies, especially food. To accomplish this, in addition to the relief plane flights, a sea or land corridor must be opened up under international control. Only this method would be able to furnish Biafrans with the six to eight thousand tons of relief supplies needed each week.

The Mission also made suggestions in the following specific areas:

- Health -- The already existing campaign for vaccination against measles and smallpox should be widened so as to include more than 50 per cent of the population and health education plans should be instituted to spread information into the more remote areas.

- Agriculture -- Relief supplies -- insecticides, seeds, baby chicks, tools, etc.--should be made available to the Land Army, Biafra's farmers' corps.

- Education -- Bombing of schools should be stopped so that children can use school buildings, as well as to avert the carrying out of intellectual genocide against the next generation.

- Transportation -- In order to insure the adequate distribution of relief supplies, tires and spare parts for cars and trucks should be supplied when required along with lubricants, gas, and vehicle repair tools.

Such was the difference in the official stand and the people's stand. The United States maintained a separation between the political and the humanitarian situations of the civil war. The Soviet Union (U.S.S.R) was involved on the Nigerian side and the United States was well aware of the influence U.S.S.R could have on Nigeria as a result of its support. This was still during the Cold

War era when the U.S. was still preoccupied with stopping the Soviet Union from spreading communism. U.S. official support for Nigeria can be based on many factors including economic factors such as trade. The U.S. stand in this case can also be looked at from the saying "keep your friends close (Britain) and your enemies closer (U.S.S.R)." Officially the capitalist Western bloc (U.S., Britain and France) found themselves on the same side as the Communist Eastern bloc (U.S.S.R) in not recognizing Biafra and supporting Nigeria in the case of the civil war.

Since the civil war, the U.S. economic interest and influence in Nigeria has grown. Nigeria had more socioeconomic and political ties with the west than the eastern nations.

USSR - Russia

The Soviet Union had little presence and influence on Nigeria prior to the war. During the war it supplied Nigeria with diplomatic support and arms on a cash and carry basis. The relationship between the two countries became a mutually beneficial one, with the Soviets gaining in-roads, economic benefits and political influence, while Nigeria got the supply of arms needed without any humanitarian conditions attached.

France

France played a flip-flop role. It supported Biafra yet it dillydallied when it came to recognizing Biafra as a sovereign nation. Officially its policy was not to recognise Biafra, but at the same time it would make official statements implying France had not ruled out recognizing Biafra. France also made a statement about resolving the war based on self-determination rights. That statement clearly supporting what Lt. Col Ojukwu claimed to be fighting for. General de Gaulle had expressed his belief that such artificial federations led to one ethnic group imposing its authority on another. Also, the French were supplying arms to Biafra. France had an axe to grind with Nigeria because she took a strong stand against France's nuclear test in the Sahara and broke diplomatic ties with her in 1961. Conversely, France had to be mindful of its economic interest in Nigeria, which also ran into millions of dollars. France was involved in Nigeria's oil industry in the Midwest, which was in Federal territory.

Such were the dilemmas that France found itself in...*to recognise or not to recognise*. Officially it stuck to not recognizing Biafra. Biafrans had expected much more from France than France was willing to give. France was, however, in the forefront when it came to the humanitarian efforts for Biafra.

Biafra

During the civil war Biafra saw herself as a sovereign nation. Colonel Ojukwu was military governor of the old Eastern Region comprising what now constitutes Rivers, Bayelsa, Cross River, Akwa-Ibom and the South-East states. Biafra was constituted from Nigeria's Eastern Region and Colonel Ojukwu became its Head of State. Biafra had a broadcasting station, Radio Biafra, which relayed rousing speeches given by Ojukwu. The breakaway nation designed her flag, had a national anthem called "Land of the rising sun," and issued her own currency, the Biafran pound. Her motto was Peace, Unity and Freedom. Biafra formed a well-structured civil service and tried to sustain herself. Ojukwu wanted the secessionist nation to be recognised internationally. Nigeria on the other hand made it clear that Biafra should not be recognised as Nigeria was one nation, including the Eastern Region. Countries found themselves walking a tight rope trying to decide what was politically, economically and morally the right thing for them to do. Among the African countries that recognised Biafra are Gabon, Zambia, Ivory Coast and Tanzania. Ghana, where the Aburi Accord was signed by both the Nigerian government and Biafran representatives, played a mediating role. Some nations, even though they did not recognise

Biafra, provided aid. Nations such as Israel, France, Portugal, Rhodesia and South Africa were in this category. The Vatican also provided support. Britain, United States and Russia as nations did not recognise Biafra, and provided humanitarian aid only after a public outcry from their citizens.

After the civil war, many Igbo emigrated to the US with their families. Their young children are now adults and have given birth to a new generation of Nigerian-Americans. Knowledge about events of the Biafran war continues to be passed down to each generation of Igbo and the new generation, although having no experience of the war, have expressed their acquired knowledge in award winning novels and plays.

Nigeria Since the war

The terrible war, in which it is estimated that more than a million lives were lost, is over but defending the defenseless in the Nigeria that emerged from that conflict is still a task that must be done. In a moment of great magnanimity, the victorious Head of State, General Yakubu Gowon, declared that henceforth there would be "neither victors nor vanquished." Nigeria no longer uses the British parliamentary system but styles its democracy after the American party system with a presidential candidate.

For most of the years between the Civil War's end in 1970 and 1999, Nigerians were ruled by military men brought to power by coups d'état. The army at last returned to the barracks after their governance had been completely discredited by the reign of General Sani Abacha. But the dividends that a return to civilian rule were thought to ensure have not yet been fully realized.

Ethnic tensions remain, as testified to by the fact that in the post war era regional administration has been abolished in favor of smaller units. Where once there were four regions there are now 36 states formed largely in response to the demands of more and more of the country's 250 ethnic groups to control a territory in which they are in the majority. Even with 36 states, there is still agitation for more states by different ethnic groups within the states. Every group feels the only way it can get part of the national revenue "pie" is by carving out a state headed by one of their own ethnic group. In the midst of this demand for more states is also a cry by some for a breakup of the country into North and South or autonomous regions.

The oil boom continues to enrich the elite rather than to alleviate the economic woes of the country's poor majority. Nigeria has natural resources enough to make it one of the world's leading emerging nations. But, instead, thanks to a corrosive culture of corruption, bad governance due to several years of military dictatorship, it languishes among the world's poorest countries. Human rights lawyer and pro-democracy activist, the late Chief Gani Fawehinmi, using the law, challenged the corrupt system. The late Afrobeat musician, Fela Anikulapo Kuti used his music to confront the corrupt military junta and their cohorts. Both men were constantly thrown in jail on trumped-up charges as were other activists that protested against military rule.

Having successfully kept Nigeria together, General Gowon was faced with a dilemma. What should post war Nigeria become. The task of the military on the battlefield was done. What should their role off it be? Was Nigeria ready to return to the civilian rule whose political chaos had spawned the Civil War? Gowon, as did each of the military rulers who succeeded him, promised to return the nation to civilian control. When or whether that promise would have been kept we will never know because he himself was ousted from power by General Murtala Muhammed in a military coup. General Murtala Muhammed was assassinated less than a year after taking over, but his pledge to hand power back to civilians was carried out by his successor, General Olusegun Obasanjo.

The elected government to whom he transferred power, was itself ousted at the beginning of its second term. The regime of

General Muhammadu Buhari and his deputy General Tunde Idiagbon often took draconian measures to clean up the corruption that had become the hallmark of the *Second Republic*. A War Against Indiscipline (WAI) was declared, but before it could also be waged against corrupt military officers, General Ibrahim Babangida overthrew the reformist regime. After eight years of rule he organized elections that were finally held in 1993. They turned out to be the freest and fairest ever conducted in Nigeria. The winner of the presidential contest was Moshood Abiola, a Yoruba Muslim from the South West. But before the results could be officially announced, Babangida annulled the election. So great was the outcry that he was forced to, as he put it, "step aside." An Interim National Government (ING) was set up headed by a Yoruba businessman, Ernest Shonekan. The real power, however, remained in the hands of the Minister of Defense, General Sani Abacha, a close ally of Babangida. After a few months the charade was ended and Shonekan was persuaded to resign and hand over power to Abacha.

The Abacha regime took crony corruption to a height never before seen. That, added to horrific human rights abuses carried out against his enemies, led to military rule being so tainted upon Abacha's sudden and mysterious death, his successor General Abdulsalami Abubakar immediately set out to return the military to the barracks. He freed most political prisoners but, giving in to pressure from those who felt that Abiola would try to reclaim his stolen mandate, left him incarcerated. There, denied the ability to seek outside medical treatment for his declining health, the winner of the famous June 12 election, died.

Abubakar organized elections and on May 29, 1999, the winner Olusegun Obasanjo, a former military ruler, returned to power not through the barrel of a gun but the ballot box. President Obasanjo would go on and serve two terms till 2007.

Dangerous storm clouds gathered under President

Umaru Yar'Adua and President Goodluck Jonathan who were democratically elected in 2007 and 2011 respectively. A fanatical Islamic sect known popularly as Boko Haram[20] unleashed a pogrom mainly in the northern part of the country. Southern Nigeria, which has taken pride in the comity that exists between Christians and Muslims, experienced some retaliatory attacks on mosques. In 2012, mosques and Islamic schools were attacked and burnt in Benin City. Newspapers reported that some Northern Muslims in Benin were seeking refuge at police stations and army barracks. Wole Soyinka in an interview with the BBC about the unrest and violence said:

> "We see the nation heading towards civil war. We know that the civil war was preceded by problems - serious killings on both sides of the regional divide,"

Home-grown terrorism, which hitherto would have been a cultural abomination, seems to have found its root. Boko Haram attacks became more frequent and vicious. As reported, burning down schools, deadly bomb attacks at motor parks in Abuja and the kidnapping of over two hundred school-girls from their secondary school in Chibok, Borno State, were some examples of the terror the group put the nation through. The abduction of the Chibok girls led to a local and international outcry through a #Bring Back Our Girls campaign. Sadly some of these girls are still missing and there is concern they may never be found unless utmost priority is given to their rescue, rehabilitation and reintegration. Boko Haram released a video saying that some of the girls had been sold as slaves while others have been married off.

The youth of Nigeria have been discounted and are disgruntled. Their unemployment rate is high. This has led to some of them

---

20   Boko Haram means Western education is forbidden

harnessing their momentum into some of the unrest that the country has experienced.

In the Niger Delta regions, militant groups like MEND (Movement for the Emancipation of Niger Delta) and many other factions are fighting for more control over the oil resources. A large proportion of the national revenue comes from oil in the Niger Delta, which has been suffering catastrophic environmental degradation.

There has long been a disconnect, between the people of Nigeria and those governing them. Some people are disillusioned and do not believe they have a stake in the country. The leaders need to avoid the danger of this agitation.

It is essential that the people find nonviolent ways to reclaim Nigeria and thus have the zeal to defend her from further decline. I refer to this in a speech I gave titled "Reclaim Nigeria" on 24, July 2010 at the launch of my husband Walter Carrington's book, *A Duty to Speak: Refusing to remain silent in a time of Tyranny*, marking his 80th birthday celebration.

> *"We must finish what was started when our fallen heroes and some of you here fought against military dictatorship to reclaim Nigeria on a democratic path.*
>
> *We have got to reclaim Nigeria, while trying to save her. Nigeria has got to belong to you the people. When Nigeria belongs to the people they will have every vested interest to save her.*
>
> *Having said that I ask of the people "Even if you feel Nigeria has not done much for you, you have much you can do for Nigeria." You can start by reclaiming what rightly belongs to you... Your country, Nigeria."*
>
> *"My husband believes in Nigeria and its potential for*

greatness just like our forefathers did. Pa Enahoro, Prof Soyinka and all our other seniors here today have been fighting the battle for Nigeria and I know they will continue to fight for her, but I believe the next generation must be prepared to take over the baton and begin to fight and defend Nigeria as vigorously as those before have been doing. You must ensure that come 2011, credible elections are held and upheld. You must begin to hold your government accountable to you the people. There must no longer be a disconnect, between the people being governed and the people governing them.

When I gave the Harvard commencement oration in 2000, I talked about Nigeria surviving the civil war but yet was still plagued with problems and I also talked about the importance of defending the defenseless. We still need to defend Nigeria as it continues to find its feet. But most importantly, Ladies and Gentlemen, what I charge you the people with today is: YOU MUST RECLAIM NIGERIA!"

The 2015 elections in which for the first time the ruling party was defeated raises hope that democracy has been further embedded in the country. However people want to feel the dividends of democracy such as jobs, a good education and an adequate healthcare system amongst other things.

Nevertheless Nigeria remains a country of great potential in all aspects. There has been an expansion of the mobile telecommunication industry, with emerging opportunities in the finance sector. Social media connects people more than ever before and with the increased cultural transmission and cross ethnic interaction that these developments bring, one hopes that Nigerians *en masse* will begin to have a vested interest in Nigeria and her future by demanding good governance and accountability. Those elected are not accountable simply to any one individual, ethnic group or party; they are accountable to the people and the nation as a whole. To achieve a nation of unity, leaders should address the Nigerian agenda and not the northern or southern agenda.

The old but very true adage that 'We are our brothers and sisters keepers' is very apt. We are interlocked and so should not be catalysts that ignite the flames of war but be the ones that extinguish such flames or at least quell them.

The complexities of Nigeria continues to captivate the minds of many. No matter how daunting the challenges are, we should love one another as one nation, one people from different ethnic backgrounds with different mother tongues and religions.

REFLECTIONS...

"Our strength lies not only in our similarities but also in our differences. *Learning to see those different from us as allies and not threats goes a long way in building coalitions."*

Our differences are what make us unique.

We must learn to love one another, listen to each other and learn from one another. It is when we love one another that we are more receptive to listen to each other and when we listen there is always something we can learn from each other.

The power of love is greater than the love of power.

"Waging war to attain peace seems like an oxymoron." *The casualties a war brings and impact it has, lingers way into the future.*

I have seen war and peace and I know: **"The bitter memory of war is difficult to erase but the sweet memory of peace is easy to embrace."**

"It is one's hope that the memory of those who lost their lives during the war, help to direct the country towards peace.

"War should on no account be encouraged."

War has no winners. It only leaves behind a trail of destruction.

"There is no such thing as a good war. A good war is an oxymoron. What are the underlying root causes? It is important to address causative factors before an incident."

There are so many questions that continue to abound as wars and disagreements break out between nations and within nations. Through all the questions one answer that should be constantly clear whether in time of war or time of peace is **'We must defend the defenseless'.** *"*

TO MY FATHER FROM DAUGHTER

You taught me about honesty,
You taught me about strength,
You taught me to be bold,
In a world that favours men.

Education meant the world to you,
As an orphan you said it was your light,
It made that difference between day and night
Education should be paramount in every child's life.

You believed in integrity,
You said hold your head up high,
Try and be above reproach,
In all aspects of life.

Community was important,
Be your neighbour's keeper you would say,
Help others when you may,
Including those you meet on the way.

Thank you for your legacy,
For values I hold dear,
Courage, Compassion and Character you always used to stress,
Defend the defenseless and all those in distress.

MEMORABLE PICTURES

Ancestral Family Pictures

Oba Ovonramwen and family in exile in Calabar

Chief Agho Obaseki (Obaseki
of Benin and Iyase of Benin),
Ovonramwen's son in law
and my great grand father

Chief Gaius Obaseki (Iyase
of Benin), my grandfather

Chief Gaius Obaseki,
my grandfather

My Parents

Dora Obaseki in the 1940s

My parent's Wedding, London

Elisha Noyoze Ukponmwan, Father

Dora Ukponmwan, Mother

Dora and Noyoze Ukpomnwan, My Parents

Residences

Masterfully Carved Lion in my childhood Ikoyi home

Parent's Family Home

Parents and Daughter

Arese and father, Noyoze Ukponmwan in Ikoyi Lagos

Arese with father at Graduation from Medical
School, University of Ibadan 1980

Arese with mother at Graduation from Medical
School, University of Ibadan 1980

Traditional Attires

**Dora Ukponmwan in Edo
Traditional Attire**

**Arese Carrington in Edo
Traditional Attire**

**Dora Ukponmwan in Yoruba
Traditional Outfit**

**Arese Carrington in Nigerian
Traditional Attire**

Naturalization, White House and U.S. Presidential Inauguration

Arese Carrington at the Immigration and Naturalization Services (INS) Office Baltimore

Dr. Arese Carrington, President Bill Clinton and Ambassador Walter Carrington in the Oval Office

Dr. Arese Carrington and Ambassador Walter Carrington

Diplomatic Functions

**Amb. Walter and Dr. Arese Carrington with
other diplomats in Abuja, Nigeria**

Arese and Walter Carrington at an Embassy Residence Concert

Arese and Walter Carrington on July
4th at Embassy Residence Lagos

Walter and Arese Carrington

President Carter's Visit to Abuja, Nigeria

The Carringtons and The Carters

Arese Carrington and Rosalynn Carter at Wuse Market, Abuja

President Carter's Visit to Enugu, Nigeria

President Jimmy Carter dressed as a Nigerian Traditional Chief

**President Carter's visit to Enugu at a parasitic
Guinea Worm contaminated water site**

NADECO Members and Other Political Pictures

Chief M.K.O. Abiola and Ambassador Walter Carrington at a reception

Ambassador Carrington and Chief Bola Ige,
Former Attorney General of Nigeria

NADECO Pro-Democracy Activists- Chief Abraham
Adesanya and Chief Gani Fawehinmi

Dr. Arese Carrington, Prof. Wole Soyinka and Amb. Walter Carrington

Farewell Party

Ambassador Carrington and Dr. Arese Carrington in traditional
attire at Farewell Party hosted by Chief and Mrs. Kuye

Chief Omowale Kuye, Dr. Arese Carrington
and Ambassador Walter Carrington

**The Carringtons at the Farewell Party Hosted by UNDP
Rep. Mr. Chinsman and Mrs. Chinsman**

Harvard Graduation and Harvard School of Public Health

Dr. Arese Carrington receiving Master of Public Health degree from Harvard University

Dr. Carrington and Nobel Prize Winner Amartya Sen at Harvard Commencement 2000

**Dr. Arese Carrington presenting The Bill and Melinda
Gates Grant Letter to President Obasanjo**

United Nations Association of Greater Boston

Arese Carrington giving a speech at UN Day Luncheon

Arese Carrington at UNAGB Gala in Boston

Dr. Arese Carrington with Boston Mayor Walsh at UNAGB Gala

Mayor Walsh, Dr. Carrington and H.E. Ban Ki Moon

UN Day Luncheon Boston

Dr. Arese Carrington with Presidents

President Bill Clinton and Dr. Arese Carrington

**Ambassador Carrington, President Carter and
Dr. Arese Carrington at Abuja Airport**

Dr. Arese Carrington and President Olusegun Obasanjo

President Jerry Rawlings and Dr. Arese Carrington

APPENDIX I

HARVARD COMMENCEMENT 2000

Around the School - May 12, 2000
HSPH Student to Speak at University Commencement

Arese Carrington

An MPH candidate who witnessed the ravages of civil war first hand in her native Nigeria has been selected to deliver the Graduate English Address at Harvard University Commencement at the Cambridge campus on June 8. Arese Ukpoma Carrington of the Department of Population and International Health was chosen from all the graduate student applicants university-wide and will speak on their behalf. She is the first HSPH student to be selected since 1993.

"We do a lot of good work at HSPH," she said. "In the 21st century, public health will be an important global issue, and Commencement will be a good platform to help people understand what public health is about."

The theme of Carrington's speech is "Defend the Defenseless," a maxim she learned from her father after the Nigerian civil war erupted in 1966. Before then, Carrington's childhood was wonderful, she said. Her father was a civil engineer, and her mother was the great-granddaughter of a former king of Benin. One of seven children, she was unaware of the mounting chaos in her country.

"When the winds of war are in the air," she said, "parents try to protect their children. We asked them, 'What is going on? Why are we seeing these images of fighting on television?'"

Carrington's parents split the family to increase their chances of survival. Her father gathered the four oldest children, leaving Carrington and her younger brother and sister in the care of their mother. Before her father departed, he offered her the words she has chosen for her platform. "He said, 'Look after your younger siblings. They are virtually defenseless. I am going to give you a duty--defend the defenseless'," she remembered.

Carrington was nine years old at the time. The words, she said, ring with her today, as do the memories of her parents' bravery.

"Even when we were hearing bombs and shelling outside," she said, "my mother would tell us that it would be okay. As children, we tend to look at our parents to see what kind of emotions we should be feeling. My mother showed great bravery."

The family was eventually reunited. Carrington later pursued a career in medicine and became a practicing physician in 1980. In 1986, she founded and served as chief executive officer of Health and Medical Services, an international consulting company specializing in preventive health care in the workplace. To avoid conflicts of interest, she gave up the company in 1995 when she married the American ambassador to Nigeria, Walter Carrington, an alumnus of Harvard Law School.

They moved to the United States when the ambassadorship was over, and Carrington reexamined her goals. The former doctor and business executive decided to enter the public health arena, coming to HSPH in 1999.

Raising awareness of public health issues in developing countries is especially important to Carrington. Now an American citizen, she hopes to put her cross-cultural perspective to work on international, public health levels.

Carrington submitted her written speech to a panel of six judges in the beginning of April. She was asked to deliver the address at a preliminary audition and then at a final audition on April 25.

Carrington also was recently elected marshal for this year's graduating class at HSPH.

Approximately 30,000 people are expected to attend Commencement exercises in Cambridge this year. Afterwards, HSPH members will return to the Longwood campus to hear speaker David Ho, *Time Magazine's* "Man of the Year" in 1996. Ho helped discover that a combination of protease inhibitors administered shortly after infection with HIV drastically reduced the amount of virus in the blood.

Around the School - June 8, 2000

MPH Student Urges Graduates at University Commencement to "Defend the Defenseless"

Arese Carrington

MPH candidate Arese Carrington was chosen to deliver the Graduate English Address at Harvard University Commencement on Thursday, June 8. The following is her speech:

As we go through life, we witness different things. I have witnessed war and peace. Of all the things that I have witnessed, the most compelling is the power of love that knows no boundaries. The most disheartening is the power of hate that builds all boundaries.

As a child I saw my family torn apart during the civil war in my native country Nigeria. My mother and father, fearful of being caught by the advancing rebel army, divided their seven children-- my father, escaping the war-torn zone with four of my siblings, my mother remaining behind with the youngest three, including me. They hoped at the worst, one-half of the family would survive to carry on. Each decision was equally dangerous, and we did not know when, if ever, we would be reunited. The night of the separation, my father had parting words for us. To my mother he said, "Be brave and tune in to the radio daily to keep abreast of the war."

He turned to me and said, "Look after your younger siblings. They are defenseless. You must defend the defenseless."

He had charged me with a duty. I could not afford to worry or think of myself. I had been given a responsibility and would be accountable to my father.

For nine agonizing months, we did not know whether they were alive or dead. Then on my mother's birthday, as we listened to the radio, we heard my father make a birthday request for her. Despite miles of war separating us, love was powerful enough to cross all those boundaries. We were given a ray of hope and joy. But that same evening, I watched over our fence as hate allowed an innocent civilian to be gunned down by soldiers because of his ethnicity.

My family and Nigeria survived that war as the country has survived many trials since then. Pursuing an academic degree at Harvard, in this relatively sheltered intellectual environment, we may easily feel removed from the realities of the world we have temporarily left behind. However heartily we may sing of *Fair Harvard,* let us never forget that there is a world out there that is anything but fair.

Had I wanted to escape, even for an academic year, the problems I every day faced as a medical doctor in Nigeria, I should have chosen another school in this university rather than the School of Public Health. There I have studied the many scourges that threaten the welfare of much of the developing world. I have also learned some of the ways to help in the remedying of them. Public health is a public good, so for it to be effective, we must have a conscience for social justice. I have learned how important it is to marshal the resources needed to finance public health programs. The United Nations and its member governments will bear most of the burden.

But I would not like to see any of you who this day will receive your graduate degrees deprived of the opportunity to contribute to the 21st-century goal of permanently dismounting three of the four horsemen of the apocalypse--war, pestilence, and hunger.

Our Harvard degree is a powerful weapon that we can use to make a difference by ensuring the principle of social justice is maintained. Graduates from all the different schools have a role to play. We each have a responsibility and will be held accountable.

To our siblings who graduate from the Business and Law Schools. As you assume your leadership roles on Wall Street and in corporate America you can relieve the guilt those large starting salaries are likely to instill in you. Contribute generously to organizations working in the deprived areas of the world. Since your offerings will be tax deductible, you can do good while doing well. But I also look to our siblings, the graduates of the Divinity School. Offer prayers that the class of 2000 may raise a standard of social consciousness to which all succeeding classes of the Third Millennium may repair.

I am now an American citizen, however I cannot ignore the plight of the land I left behind. The significance of the words of my late father encompasses so much. His words ring in my ears, "You must defend the defenseless."

Around the School
is published weekly by the Office of Communications
Harvard School of Public Health
665 Huntington Ave., 1204
Boston, Massachusetts 02115
617-432-6052, 617-432-6052
Editor: Christina Roache
Photo Credits: Richard Chase

Around the School - June 16, 2000
Congratulations to Class of 2000

Arese Carrington, MPH graduate, delivered the Graduate English Address at Commencement exercises in Cambridge on Thursday, June 8. More than 300 students of HSPH graduated on Thursday, June 8. Of the graduates, more than 265 received master's degrees and more than 50 received doctoral degrees. The students hailed from 34 countries.

Renowned AIDS researcher David Ho was HSPH's principal Commencement speaker.

Nobel laureate Amartya Sen, adjunct professor in the Department of Population and International Health, gave the principal address in Cambridge.

Around the School
is published weekly by the Office of Communications
Harvard School of Public Health
665 Huntington Ave., 1204
Boston, Massachusetts 02115
617-432-6052 , 617-432-6052
Editor: Christina Roache
Photo Credits: Christopher Ternan, Justin Ide/Harvard News Office

The Harvard University Gazette
June 15, 2000
Harvard Gazette Archives

Time of their lives

Some glimpses from a very special day
Notable quote from the Graduate English Address
"You must defend the defenseless."

– Arese Ukpoma Carrington

http://news.harvard.edu/gazette/2000/06.15/commencecolor.html

---

The Harvard Crimson

June 23, 2000

Amid Pageantry, 6,165 Graduates Receive Degrees

Harvard Yard swells with proud family members
By William P. Bohlen and Imtiyaz H. Delawala,
CRIMSON STAFF WRITERS

Dr. Arese U. Carrington, a graduating student from the School of Public Health, inspired the crowd with her call for students to "defend the defenseless" in her Graduate English Address. Carrington's family was divided during civil war in her native country of Nigeria, leaving her and her mother to care for Carrington's younger siblings for nine months.

http://www.thecrimson.com/article/2000/6/23/
amid-pageantry-6165-graduates-receive-degrees/?print=1

John Harvard's Journal

Commencement Confetti

An omnium-gatherum of notes and statistics, vital and otherwise

TALK, A SAMPLER.....

A survivor of civil war in her native Nigeria and a candidate for a master's degree in public health delivered the Graduate English Address at the Commencement exercises. During the war, when she was nine, said Arese Ukpoma Carrington, her father told her, "Look after your younger siblings. They are defenseless. You must defend the defenseless." "Defend the defenseless," Carrington exhorted her audience. **"Of all the things that I have witnessed, the most compelling is the power of love that knows no boundaries. The most disheartening is the power of hate that builds all boundaries."**

http://harvardmagazine.com/2000/07/
commencement-confetti.html

Protocol

SPECIAL COMMENCEMENT ISSUE

Vol. 5 Number 3

Spring 2000

Graduate English Address   "Defend the Defenseless"

Dr. Arese Ukpoma Carrington, a candidate for the MPH degree in the Department of Population and International Health at the School of Public Health, is also a Class Marshal. A physician by training, Dr. Carrington decided to change from curative to preventive medicine to address public health problems. Originally from Nigeria, she bases her speech on her childhood experiences during civil war there. After her marriage to the former American Ambassador to Nigeria, Walter Carrington, she came to America and began her studies at Harvard. Her future plans include working on public policy issues affecting health care. She is also a collector and cataloguer of African art.

Left to Right: Kathleen Sietsko, Justin Krebs, Dr. Arese Carrington, Professor Richard Thomas

HARVARD UNIVERSITY

On Thursday, June 8, 2000, Harvard student
Dr. Arese Ukpoma Carrington
delivered a short address at the Harvard Commencement before
30,000 students, faculty, alumni, and guests. This certificate
affirms her wisdom, wit, and eloquence on this joyous day of
endings and beginnings.

Professor Richard Thomas
Chairman, Commencement Parts

Richard M. Hunt
University Marshal

Harvard University Commencement Address Certificate

NEWS CAPTIONS ON GRADUATE ORATION

The Harvard Crimson
THURSDAY, JUNE 8, 2000

SPH's Carrington Urges Graduates To 'Defend the Defenseless'

By BARBARA E. MARTINEZ
CRIMSON STAFF WRITER

Dr. Arese Carrington, the School of Public Health (SPH) student who speaks this morning as the graduate English orator, will urge her listeners to "Defend the Defenseless"—a message she learned from her father during the Nigerian Civil War in the 1960s.

Carrington, who is 41, has devoted her life's work to fulfilling this maxim, earning an M.D. in 1980 and a master's degree from SPH today.

TELL, June 12, 2000

People
Arese Walks Tall

In a rare acknowledgement of her talents and leadership roles, Arese, wife of Walter Carrington, former US ambassador to Nigeria, delivers a graduation oration at Harvard University where she also bags a postgraduate degree in Public Health

June 15, 2000 **Harvard University Gazette** • 9

Moments in history

(Continued from previous page)

Notable quote from the Graduate English Address
"You must defend the defenseless."
— Arese Ukpoma Carrington

THE BOSTON GLOBE • FRIDAY, JUNE 9, 2000

The morning ceremony featured a fellow graduate, Arese Ukpoma Carrington. A survivor of Nigeria's civil war who later became a doctor and married a US ambassador, she urged students to work for social justice and promote public health throughout the world.

The address she is going to deliver this week derives its title, "Defend the Defenceless" from one of Arese's father's favourite maxims. "I learnt it from my father after the Nigerian civil war erupted in 1966," she said.

Like her husband who used his position as the US ambassador to Nigeria to fight on the side of the cheated, the oppressed and the marginalised masses of the country, Arese's weapon lies in the health sciences. In an interview with a Lagos-based daily last year, the Benin-born physician declared: "When we talk about democracy in the life of a people, I believe that the health, in other words, lives of the people comes first. Having attained a commendable height in her quest for a healthy society. She got married to Carrington in 1995. And when the ambassadorial tenure of this social crusader expired in 1997, the couple relocated to the US.

The Guardian Online - http://www.ngrguardiannews.com
Thursday, June 8, 2000

Arese, Carrington's Nigerian wife speaks at Havard today

WIFE of former American ambassador to Nigeria, Arese Ukpoma Carrington, will today in Cambridge, deliver an address on promotion of public health and social justice, at Harvard

President Clinton's congratulations letter on commencement speech

THE WHITE HOUSE

WASHINGTON

August 18, 2000

Dr. Arese Carrington

�█████ █████

████████████████████████

Dear Arese:

Thanks for your kind letter and the copy of your speech. You can be very proud of all you have accomplished so far.

I'm pleased that your address focused on the importance of "defending the defenseless." Our world needs people like you and Walter who are dedicated to bringing hope and help to those who are less fortunate, and I commend you for conveying this powerful message to your class-mates at Harvard. My Administration has worked hard to expand economic prosperity and promote democracy around the globe, goals which I will again highlight on my trip to Nigeria later this month.

As we continue our efforts in this area, I hope you will remain involved. Best wishes to you and your family for continued success and every happiness.

Sincerely,

Bill Clinton

Senator Kennedy's congratulations letter on being selected as commencement speaker:

Edward M. Kennedy
Massachusetts

United States Senate
WASHINGTON, DC 20510

June 8, 2000

Dr. Arese Carrington, MD

Dear Arese:

I am delighted to extend my warmest congratulations on your selection as graduate student orator for the 2000 Harvard Commencement.

This is a prestigious honor and I am especially pleased by the theme that you have chosen for your address as we begin this new century. To echo the noble call of your father to "Defend the Defenseless" demonstrates that as a physician and graduate of the Harvard School of Public Health, you intend to champion the important cause of quality health care for all peoples in all nations.

I encourage you to continue to be a bold voice on behalf of the millions of adults and children around the world who desperately need good health care and who will benefit immensely from better delivery of health services and advances in health research.

I share these high priorities, and I commend you for your commitment. With best wishes in the years ahead,

Sincerely,

Edward M. Kennedy

Edward M. Kennedy
Washington, D. C. 20002

APPENDIX II

HARVARD SCHOOL OF PUBLIC HEALTH
GATES FOUNDATION GRANT

Around the School - May 12, 2000

HSPH Student to Speak at University Commencement

**HSPH Receives $25 Million From Gates Foundation
to Prevent Spread of AIDS in Nigeria**

An initiative of HSPH to prevent the spread of HIV and AIDS in Nigeria has received $25 million from the Bill and Melinda Gates Foundation. The grant is the largest single private grant awarded to HSPH in its history and the second given to HSPH by the Gates Foundation in two months. The grant will fund the Nigerian AIDS Prevention Initiative, a program sponsored by HSPH in collaboration with the Harvard Center for International Development at the Kennedy School of Government.

HSPH alumna Arese Carrington, who graduated last spring, expedited the initial planning stage of the proposal. A native of Nigeria and wife of the former US ambassador to the country, Carrington was able to put HSPH representatives in touch quickly with key officials in her homeland, including Nigerian president Olusegun Obasanjo.

Carrington is associate director of the initiative, a job she feels matches her goals in public health to her desire to help people in developing countries. HSPH members may remember that Carrington was chosen to deliver the Harvard University graduate student commencement address last June.

Carrington will also serve as liaison between HSPH and the Nigerian Advisory Council, established through the initiative. The council will include representatives from Nigeria's National Assembly and National Committee on AIDS, as well as from scientific and business communities. They will guide all aspects of planning and oversee administration of the initiative in Nigeria.

http://www.hsph.harvard.edu/ats/Nov17/

This Day

Nigeria: Arese Carrington: Stalking The AIDS

11 December 2000

Lagos — A childhood vision of care led her into medicine. Now, Dr. (Mrs.) Arese Carrington visits the country, at the behest of Harvard School of Public Health (HSPH), to present to the Federal Government a letter confirming a $25 million grant by the Bill & Melinda Gates Foundation, to HSPH, to kick-off a collaborative AIDS prevention offensive in Nigeria. Louis Achi and Mike Jimoh report

"I am now an American citizen, however I cannot ignore the plight of the land I left behind. The significance of the words of my late father encompasses so much. His words ring in my ears - 'you must defend the defenseless.'" The foregoing, an excerpt from the 2000 Harvard Graduation Oration, delivered in June, by Nigerian-born Dr. (Mrs.) Arese Ukpoma Carrington, wife of former US ambassador to Nigeria, Walter Carrington, encapsulates much of the philosophy that has driven her life.

http://allafrica.com/stories/200012110337.html

The Washington Times-Nigeria gets a $25 million grant from Harvard University

The Washington Times

Originally published 12:00 a.m., December 13, 2000, updated 12:00 a.m., December 13, 2000

Embassy Row

Nigeria gets AIDS grant

Nigeria yesterday received a $25 million grant from Harvard University to fight AIDS, the wife of the former U.S. ambassador to Nigeria announced.

Arese Carrington, a director of the Harvard School of Public Health, said the money will be released in grants of $5 million apiece over the next 18 months.

Walter Carrington was ambassador there from 1993 to 1997.

http://www.washingtontimes.com/news/2000/
dec/13/20001213-013503-3475r/print/

APPENDIX III

SELECT FAREWELL LETTERS AND INVITATIONS

Walter Carrington's Send - Off Planning Committee

C/O Senator Abraham Adesanya

12, Simpson Street, Lagos. Tel: 2634052, 2647272

Our Ref.: WCSPC/09/97

Monday, September 8, 1997

**His Excellency
Mr. Walter Carrington**
Ambassador of the United States
of America to Nigeria,
Embassy of the United States of America,
3, Eleke Crescent,
Victoria Island,
Lagos.

Your Excellency,

SEND - OFF PARTY

In recent times, our dear country, Nigeria, has witnessed very turbulent moments, particularly after the unwarranted annulment of the June 12, 1993 Presidential Election by the military junta. In their quest to redress this military-imposed anomaly, Nigerians embarked on series of mass actions internally and also solicited for the assistance of the international community.

In recognition of the laudable roles that you and your country, the United States of America have played in the struggle to restore democracy in Nigeria, all human rights, pro-democracy groups and political activists met on Wednesday, September 3, 1997 at the Chambers of Senator Abraham Adesanya and agreed to organise a befitting send-off party for you to mark the end of your very successful tenure in Nigeria.

In furtherance of the above, we write to inform you that there will be a send-off party for you on Thursday, September 18, 1997 at the residence of Pa Solanke Onasanya at 3 Ore Close, via Ogunlana Drive, Surulere, Lagos at 6.00p.m.

With highest regards.

Yours sincerely,

SEN. ABRAHAM ADESANYA
Chairman Planning Committee

EBUN-OLU ADEGBORUWA
Secretary Planning Committee.

THE TRIUMPHANT CHORALE
(VOICES)

Our Ref: CF/FC/Vol.9/97

Your Ref:..........................

P.O.Box 3957
Ikoyi, Lagos

4TH OCT., 1997

Your Excellency,

A SPECIAL FAREWELL VISIT

Peace be with you!. We, members of the above group wish to pay His Excellency and the spouse (family) a special Farewell Visit to formally acknolwedge your immense and unequalled contributions to our Political developments more than any known U.S Ambassador to Nigeria. TIME is 4 - 5pm, Sunday, 5th October, 1997.

The Triumphants earnestly believe in you and your spouse, but regret our inability to prove this quantifiably. Not to worry, as our hearts of love will prayerfully recount this, all is well in Jesus.

As we live, we keep on trotting the globe. Having chosen Nigeria, of all other countries of the world as your matrimonial base, that is the height of love you have for us, as we will forever be meeting till we bid this world adieu.

With high regards, Your Excellency.

God Bless you!.

Yours faithfully,

THE OBAFEMI AWOLOWO FOUNDATIO

28 LANRE AWOLOKUN ROAD,
GBAGADA PHASE II
P.M.B. 80075 VICTORIA ISLAND,
LAGOS-STATE.
TEL / FAX: 234-1-821372

29th September, 1997

His Excellency Dr Walter Carrington
Embassy of the United States of America
2, Eleke Crescent
Victoria Island

Dear Sir,

APPRECIATION AND FAREWELL MESSAGE

The Obafemi Awolowo Foundation seizes the opportunity of your departure from Nigeria to express our profound gratitude to you for your facilitatory role in providing assistance to the Foundation throughout your tenure.

Your support, though never in doubt, was always so eloquently demonstrated by your presence at several of our outreach programmes. You have been to us a friend indeed. We wish to assure you that your name shall remain indelible in the annals of the Foundation.

Undoubtedly, you will have cause to return to Nigeria from time to time in the years ahead, thanks to your charming wife. We, therefore, look forward to your continued interest and to welcoming you to some of the Foundation's programmes in future.

We hope that the gifts accompanying this letter will serve as a constant reminder to you of the Obafemi Awolowo Foundation, and of course, Nigeria.

Please accept our best wishes to you, your wife and entire family for the future.

Yours sincerely
FOR: OBAFEMI AWOLOWO FOUNDATION

DR O. AWOLOWO DOSUMU
EXECUTIVE SECRETARY

26, Festival Road,
Victoria Island
Lagos.
Tel: 614070

FAREWELL LUNCHEON PARTY IN HONOR OF A GREAT FRIEND OF NIGERIA - AMBASSADOR WALTER C. CARRINGTON

For the past four years and some months now, a great and faithful friend of Nigeria, as well as a dedicated and loyal servant of his Country, has worked assiduously in the interest of both Nigeria and the United States of America.

Regrettably, Ambassador Walter C. Carrington and his wife are leaving, but fortunately, for green pastures at Harvard University - the peak of academic excellence.

Dr. L. A. Fabunmi will be more than delighted if you are able to honor him with your presence at a **FAREWELL LUNCHEON PARTY** in honor of His Excellency Walter C. Carrington and his wife (Dr. Arese Carrington) at 26, Festival Road, Victoria Island, Lagos, on **SATURDAY, SEPTEMBER 13TH, 1997. TIME: 1.00 P.M.**

R. S. V. P.
Tel: 614070

Human Rights activist, Chief Gani Fawehinmi's Letter of Appreciation

To   THURSDAY 16 – 10 – 2008
His Excellency And Mrs WALTER CARRING To

From
CHIEF AND MRS GANI FAWEHINMI
We will always cherish the memory
of your outstanding and extremely
courageous contribution to the
upliftment and advancement of
fundamental Human Rights in the
face of brutal and despotic
military dictatorship in Nigeria
when you were the United States
of America Ambassador in Nigeria
1993 – 1997. Our family will always remember
the concern of both of you (ARESE and
WALTER) through your prayers, telephone
calls, advice, visits etc regarding the
cancer ailment of chief Gani Fawehinmi
God Almighty will reward you and your
entire family abundantly with blessings,
protection and guidance.
– Gani Fawehinmi   G. Fawel...

APPENDIX IV

BIOGRAPHIES

ABOUT WALTER CARRINGTON (THE AUTHOR'S SPOUSE)

Humanitarian/ International Player

Walter Carrington's involvement with Africa began more than fifty years ago as a member of the United States delegation to an international youth conference in Senegal. A few years later, in 1959, on the eve of the country's Independence, he led a group of students on a program called The Experiment in International Living where they spent a summer living with Nigerian families in Lagos, Ibadan, Enugu, Port Harcourt, Kano and Kaduna. On that occasion and on subsequent visits when he was an official of the Peace Corps he met many of Founding Fathers of the country.

A civil rights activist during his university days at Harvard University, Carrington was the first student elected to the National Board of Directors of the NAACP (National Association for the Advancement of Colored People). A graduate of Harvard College (1952) and Harvard Law School (1955), Carrington practiced law in Massachusetts and served on the three- member Massachusetts Commission Against Discrimination becoming, at the age of 27, the youngest person to be appointed a commissioner in the state's history.

Carrington returned to Africa in 1961 as one of the first overseas Directors of the Peace Corps. In 1967 he had the responsibility of evacuating the young Americans as Biafran troops were advancing towards Benin. He paid courtesy calls to military governors of States to evaluate the safety and well-being of Peace Corps volunteers. Brigadier Adeyinka Adebayo assured him of the safety of the volunteers in the West and expressed profuse thanks for their good work. They remained in most parts of Nigeria throughout the war.

After the Peace Corps, Carrington's professional career continued to revolve around Africa. He became a highly respected American specialist on Africa and America's policy toward the Continent. In the 1970s, as Executive Vice President of the African-American Institute in Washington D.C. he oversaw programs that provided scholarships to hundreds of Nigerians for study in the United States. He served as publisher of the Institute's magazine, *Africa Report*, which was then the leading publication on African affairs in the United States. He reported on Nigeria's post-war efforts of reconstruction and rehabilitation. He later taught African Politics and American Foreign Policy at several universities in the United States. He has written and lectured widely on Africa and on the status of African-Americans in the United States and hosted a television series, *The African World.* He has worked on African issues as a top staff aid in the U.S. Congress and at the leading African-American think-tank, the Joint Center for Political and Economic Studies in Washington, DC.

In 1980, President Jimmy Carter appointed Carrington as Ambassador to Senegal. At the end of his service there President Diouf conferred upon him the national award of Commander in the Order of the Lion. 1n 1993, President Bill Clinton appointed him Ambassador to Nigeria. Carrington arrived in Lagos a few months after the annulment of what was regarded at the time as the freest and fairest election ever held in Nigeria. The annulment caused great unrest and regional and tribal resentment, finally leading to Babaginda handing power over to a civilian interim President, Ernest Shonekan. Carrington arrived just in time to be the last diplomat to present his credentials to the new president because two weeks later General Sani Abacha removed Shonekan in a bloodless coup.

In the four years he served as Ambassador of the United States to Nigeria, Walter Carrington was an outspoken champion of human rights and Nigeria's return to democracy and civilian rule. In spite of threats to his person and family, which included assassination attempts, Carrington continued to call for the end of military rule throughout his tour in Nigeria and after returning to the United States.

In speech and deed, he fearlessly confronted the regime of Sani Abacha, urging the United States to impose stricter sanctions on his regime. Carrington constantly called for the release of political prisoners and, when his calls went unheeded, provided comfort to the families of the detained. He was a most uncommon diplomat who openly identified with the persecuted citizens of Nigeria rather than with the unelected military cabal which persecuted them. Nigerians felt few, if any, foreigners have so consistently identified with the aspirations of the Nigerian people as did this African-American, fondly known as Omowale – "the child who has returned." After his tour of duty in Nigeria ended, Carrington continued to remain involved, doing his best to enable the country to return to democratic rule.

Upon the restoration of civilian rule in 1999, the area in Lagos on which the American and a dozen other diplomatic missions are located was renamed "Walter Carrington Crescent." In 2003 President Olusegun Obasanjo conferred upon him the national honor award of "Officer of the Federal Republic (OFR)." In 2010 Governor Babatunde Fashola of Lagos hosted a State banquet in honor of Carrington's eightieth birthday. Human Rights groups and Pro-democracy activist also put together a book of tributes to celebrate his birthday.

In his honor, in 2011 the United States consulate in Lagos established the Carrington Youth Fellowship Initiative, (CYFI). It is described as follow on the embassy website: (http://nigeria.usembassy.gov/cyfi.html)

> The Carrington Youth Fellowship Initiative, CYFI, is a dynamic youth-based initiative launched in 2011 by the U.S. Consulate General, Lagos. CYFI brings together Nigerian youth of exceptional vision, skills and experience to design and implement projects that have a positive impact on Nigerian society. Former Ambassador to Nigeria, Walter Carrington, was a champion of civil liberties, democracy and closer ties between the U.S. and Nigeria. CYFI fellows are committed to putting the ideals of Walter Carrington into practice.

Today Ambassador Carrington is an Associate of Harvard's DuBois Institute while working on a book on Nigeria and another on Islam in Africa. A collection of his Nigerian speeches, *A Duty to Speak: Refusing to Remain Silent in a Time of Tyranny,* was published in Nigeria in 2010 and launched as part of his birthday celebrations. Fully aware of the difficulties the country still faces, he continues to look forward to a stable Nigeria that will eventually harness its potential and take its place as one of the great countries of the world.

ABOUT ARESE CARRINGTON (THE AUTHOR)

Dr. Arese Carrington is a medical doctor, an international Public Health consultant and a Human Rights activist. She specializes in public health programming, women's issues and investment promotion in Africa. She previously worked as an Associate Director of the Harvard School of Public Health's AIDS Prevention Initiative in Nigeria (APIN).

Dr. Carrington's childhood vision to help others led her to become a medical doctor. She graduated from University College Hospital (UCH) Ibadan in 1980 and later founded Health and Medical Services and served as CEO. She provided practical and Advisory services on preventive health care in industrial and other environments including some diplomatic missions within Nigeria. At a time when preventive healthcare of workers was being overlooked she brought it to the forefront and put policies in place that ensured their needs were met.

During some of Nigeria's darkest hours, in spite of pressure and threats to her and her family she joined her husband Ambassador Carrington in the fight for democracy and human rights.

Upon leaving Nigeria Dr. Carrington obtained a Masters of Public Health from Harvard. While there she was elected as class marshal and was also selected to represent all of the University's graduate schools as the graduate orator at Harvard's 2000 commencement. Dr. Carrington delivered an oration summoning that year's graduates to make the problems of the developing world a high priority in their lives. Recalling the injunction her father had given her during the Nigerian Civil War she called upon the audience to "Defend the Defenseless."

She decided to switch from curative to preventive medicine in order to more effectively deal with the public health problems facing the developing world. As Associate Director of Harvard's AIDS prevention initiative in Nigeria program she was responsible for creating the conditions which led the Bill and Melinda Gates Foundation to give a $25 million dollar grant to fight HIV/AIDS in Nigeria. This was the first major grant Nigeria got for HIV/AIDS and was a major factor in attracting other donors.

She is a public speaker in America and internationally. Dr. Carrington has been a featured speaker at universities in the U.S. including her Alma mater. She was invited to speak at Harvard's Class of 52 symposium where she was the only female on a high level panel which consisted of a Nobel Prize winner, the former head of State of Jamaica, distinguished politicians and ambassadors. She spoke about "AIDS Africa's greatest scourge". With her speech she made sure she generated an interest and debate on ways Africa can be assisted. She often leaves her audience with these burning words and challenge that she holds dearly. "We cannot let Africa drown in an ocean of despair but must help her swim to the shore of hope."

In her various activities she is helping Africa swim to the shore of Hope. During the height of the Ebola pandemic in some countries in West Africa she was a vocal advocate in speeches and television interviews requesting Western help for the affected countries.

Dr. Carrington serves on the Boards of Directors and committees of several organizations. She is an Advisory Trustee board member of Beth Israel Deaconess Medical Center where she sits on the Nutrition committee and the community Benefits committee. She is Vice President of the United Nations Association of Greater Boston. UNA-GB is one of the most active and innovative supporters of the United Nations in the country. She also passionately supports the educational program of the organization in the inner city schools. She has used her role on the board to keep the focus on the plight of the abducted Chibok school girls in Nigeria through #bring back our girls activities.

Dr. Carrington is a member of the Museum of Fine Art's Visiting Committee for the Arts of Asia, Oceania and Africa. A descendant of Oba Ovonranwen who ruled the Benin Kingdom in the 19th century, she played a pivotal role in the opening of the MFA's Benin Kingdom Gallery. She is an avid collector of African art especially Benin Bronzes.

As a member of the Board of the Pan African Health Foundation (PAHF, USA) she played a major role in helping the Foundation establish Africa's first major auto disable syringe factory in Port Harcourt which was a technical breakthrough in helping to fight the AIDS pandemic in Nigeria.

She also played a key role on the board of FATE USA where she helped to screen young business school interns that go to Nigeria to mentor young entrepreneurs. At its inception, on the Advisory board of LYNX (Linking Youth in Nigeria through eXchange), she helped set up the program that was used by Nigerian undergraduates in the U.S. to put together a summer camp in Abuja for youth from all over Nigeria. These two organizations are now well established and run by youth within Nigeria.

She received the 2014 Newton Human Rights Lifelong Advocate Award. She also received citations from the Massachusetts Senate and from the Massachusetts House of Representatives for her lifelong work as a Human rights advocate within her community and worldwide.

BIBLIOGRAPHY

Blum, Jeffery D. (1969) Article in Harvard Crimson

Coleman, James S. (1958) Nigeria – Background to Nationalism, published by University of California Press

Davidson Basil (1964).The African Past, published by Longman

de St. Jorre, John. (1972). The Brothers' War - Biafra and Nigeria, Boston: Houghton Mifflin Company,

Egharevba, Chief Jacob U. (MBE) (1956). A selected record of events

Egharevba, Chief Jacob U. (MBE) (1965). Chronicle of events in Benin

Egharevba, Chief Jacob U. (MBE) (1968). A short History of Benin: Ibadan University Press

Egharevba, Chief Jacob U. (MBE) (1969). Some Prominent Benin People

Egharevba, Chief Jacob U. (MBE). Benin Titles

Igbafe, P.A. (1979). Benin under British Administration

Jinadu, L. Adele. (1974). Research in Race and Ethnic Relations, Vol 7, pages 191-231, Ethnicity, External interventions and local conflicts: The case of the Nigerian civil war.

Leith-Ross, Sylvia. (1983). Stepping-Stones: Memoirs of Colonial Nigeria 1907-1960, with introduction by Michael Crowder, London: Peter Owen.

"Nigerian Civil War." - *New World Encyclopedia*. http://www.newworldencyclopedia.org/entry/Nigerian_Civil_War

Niven, C.R. (1957). A short history of Nigeria: Longmans, Green and Co

Ryder A.F.C. (1969) Benin and the Europeans 1485-1897, published by Longmans

Siollun, Max. (2005). The Inside Story of Nigeria's First Military Coup (I)

Siollun, Max. (2006). The Inside Story of Nigeria's First Military Coup (2)

Uche, Chibuike. (2008). Oil, British interest and the Nigerian civil war. Journal of African History, 49 (2008), pp. 111–35. 2008 Cambridge University Press

Ugowe, C.O.O. (1997), Benin in World History, Hugo Books

http://www.thecrimson.com/article/1969/2/25/who-cares-about-biafra-anyway-pithis/

http://countrystudies.us/nigeria/39.htm